ALL BREATHING LIFE
ADORES YOUR NAME

At The Interface Between Poetry And Prayer

Rabbi Zalman Schachter-Shalomi

ALL BREATHING LIFE
ADORES YOUR NAME

At The Interface Between Poetry And Prayer

Translations and Compositions of
Jewish Sacred Literature
Edited by
Michael L. Kagan

Foreword
Rabbi Lawrence Kushner

Gaon Books
P.O. Box 23924
Santa Fe, NM 87502
www.gaonbooks.com

Library of Congress Cataloging-in-Publication Data
Schachter-Shalomi, Zalman, 1924-
*All breathing life : at the interface between poetry and prayer :
translations and compositions of Jewish sacred literature* / by Zalman
Schachter-Shalomi ; edited by Michael L. Kagan ; with a foreword
by Lawrence Kushner. -- 1st ed.
    p. cm.
ISBN 978-1-935604-21-1 (cloth binding : alk. paper) -- ISBN 978-1-
935604-29-7 (pbk. : alk. paper) -- ISBN 978-1-935604-30-3 (e-book)
1. Piyutim--Translations into English. 2. Jewish religious poetry,
Hebrew--Translations into English. I. Kagan, Michael L. II. Title.
BM670.P5S33 2011
296.4'52--dc23
                                                    2011023986

Manufactured in the United States of America.
The paper used in this publication is acid free and meets all
ANSI (American National Standards for Information Sciences)
standards for archival quality paper. All wood product
components used in this book are Sustainable Forest Initiative
(SFI) certified.

Contents

VI. Songs of the Rabbis

VII. An Assortment

VIII. The Songs of David

IX. And in Conclusion

X. The Master's Voice

Foreword

Kuzu b'mukh-sooz kuza
Gibberish and Poetry

Zalman insists that the poems in this volume are not translations. They are, instead, free verse evocations of themes and imagery inspired by our liturgy and collective psyche. Their nuance marks the intersection of an often indecipherable tradition and contemporary life. They bring what might otherwise be lost into the light of everyday spirituality.

After all, that is what Zalman does, who he is. He takes old Jewish stuff (legend, mime, gibberish, and gesture) that people either didn't know existed or...didn't know what to do with it, and slips it back into our back pockets when we're not looking. And then we say, months, years later: "Oh, yes, Zalman taught me how to (sing, pray, meditate on, dance, understand) do that. Indeed, Zalman has been doing that for almost three generations of otherwise rootless and assimilated American Jewish spiritual seekers. He is our way "back in" and "back home." And these poems are a complete set of VIP entry passes.

To move so effortlessly between two cultures requires placing one's feet in both—simultaneously. But that is supposed to be impossible. Any culture is, by definition, a universal set of symbols and meanings which claim to exhaust reality. This is why anthropologists remind us that people can only do one culture at a time. Not Zalman. Our *rebbe* inhabits both: Classical Ḥasidut and Contemporary America. Any lesser soul would, long ago, have split in half. Maybe this is what the early Ḥasidim meant when they claimed their *rebbe* routinely visited Heaven. Permit me an example.

Many Jews know that the *klaf* (the piece of parchment) rolled up inside a *mezuzah* case contains its own instructions: "... And you shall inscribe them [that is: these very words] on the doorposts of your house and upon your gates." They also know that, in addition to this first paragraph of the *Sh'ma'*, there is also a *Shaddai*, with a large letter *shin* scribed on the other side of the *klaf*, placed in such a way that, when rolled up, the *shin* appears on the outside at the top.

But there's another phrase that's also on every *klaf* in every *mezuzah*. It's on the back (beneath the *shin*) at the bottom. Many Jews aren't even aware of its presence. And, if they have noticed it, they don't know what it means. Indeed, I'm not even sure where one could look it up.

The phrase has three words, written in Hebrew letters. But whatever it says is not in Hebrew. It's not Aramaic either. Actually, it's not in any language. It's pure gibberish! Three words, fourteen letters: *Kaf, vav, zayin, vav. Bet, mem, vav, khaf, samekh, zayin.* And then, *Kaf, vav, zayin* and *vav* are repeated. I suppose you could pronounce it: *Kuzu b'mukh-sooz kuzu.* Don't take my word for it. Check out your own *mezuzot* for yourself. (It's probably time you checked the *k'lafim* for weather or bug damage anyway.)

The reason it's initially unintelligible is because it's in code. (What a perfect metaphor for sacred tradition!) This particular code is a Caesar cipher. In Hebrew such a code is called *AV-GaD (aleph-bet, gimel-dalet)* – one of several systems of encoding Hebrew. For example, there is *Gematria* wherein each Hebrew letter becomes a number based on its sequential place in the Hebrew alphabet. Or there is: *AT-BaSH (aleph-tav, bet-shin)* wherein every letter becomes the letter it would have been were the order of the *Aleph-Bet* reversed, i.e. *aleph* (the first letter) becomes *tav* (the last letter); *bet* (the second letter) becomes *shin* (the second from the last letter) and so forth.

Our phrase, *kuzu b'mukh-sooz kuzu*, is encoded by *AV-GaD*. In this system, each letter of the *Aleph-Bet* becomes the next letter of the Hebrew alphabet: thus, *aleph* becomes *bet* and *gimel* becomes *dalet* (hence: *AV-GaD*) and so on. (This is, by the way, is the same mechanism by which the computer in Stanley Kubrick's movie *2001: A Space Odyssey*, gets its name: HAL. It's an English version of *AV-GaD*. See if you can figure out the real name.)

Through a decoding lens of *AV-GaD, Kuzu b'mukh-sooz kuza* becomes *Adonai Eloheynu Adonai*, "the Lord, our God, is the Lord"—

the third, fourth and fifth words, respectively, of the *Sh'ma'*.
As Zalman once explained it to me, so many Jews were adding
inscriptions, incantations, and conjurings of their own invention,
there arose a danger that the *mezuzah*'s words might become
obscured or even lost. So the Rabbis decided that *kuzu b'mukh-sooz
kuzu* was to be the only permitted "secret" addition.

(Zalman once playfully suggested that we could put the phrase
above the ark and connect it to an audiometer able to read the
decibel level of prayer in the room. In this way, when the davening
reached a loud enough level, the *Kuzu b'mukh-sooz kuza* would
revert to *Adonai Eloheynu Adonai*, "the Lord, our God, is the Lord."
But that's a whole other story for another time.)

The tradition, it occurs to me, especially for many twentieth
and twenty-first century American Jews, is a lot like *kuzu b'mukh-
sooz kuzu*. We didn't notice it and, if we did, we don't know how
to read it and, if we do, we don't know what it means. It's not the
sort of thing one can simply "look up," either because we don't
know its syntax and idioms or, often, because it is not even written
down anywhere. It requires a de-coder, if you will, a teacher, a
translator.

You might say that Zalman has shown the past few generations
of us how to poetically decode the apparent gibberish of sacred
tradition into meaningful and holy words: *Kuzu b'mukh-sooz kuzu—*
The Lord, our God, is God. We are all in our *rebbe*'s debt.

Rabbi Lawrence Kushner
San Francisco, 2011

A Word from the Editor

n the summer of 2001, my family and I packed up our
Jerusalem home and moved to Boulder, Colorado for a
two-year stay. Why we left Israel, we were not sure. Why
we decided on Boulder was clear – Reb Zalman. A few days after we
arrived and settled in, my wife – Ruth Gan Kagan – and I had our first
meeting with him. We had met him before during one of his trips
to Israel in the late 90's. I had been teaching what I called "Holistic
Judaism" for several years – thinking that I was doing cutting-edge
stuff, exploring the bodily, emotional, mental, and spiritual inter-
faces via the festival cycle and biblical narratives – when I discovered that Reb Zalman had developed the techniques and intercon-
nections for transformation at least thirty years earlier. Now we sat
opposite him in his below-ground study a stone's throw from the
Flatirons – the first uplift of the great Rocky Mountains – grappling
with the question: Why are we here? For my wife, this question led
to the realization that everything pointed in one direction – to become a Jewish Renewal Rabbi under Reb Zalman's tutelage. For me
I had no clear answer, so I replied: *Teyn ḥelki b'Torah-tekha,* "Give me
my portion in your Torah."

And so over the next two years, I probed and listened and
learned until it became clear – Sacred Poems. For besides Reb
Zalman's wish to have Jewish sacred verse more available to the
general English language readership, this collection is a perfect
window through which to catch a glimpse at the inner workings
of a living *Rebbe*, and through this living *Rebbe*'s window, to catch
a glimpse at the myriad Rebbes and rabbis who came before.
These personalities, whom we barely know through their written
words, suddenly come alive when looked at through such a living
soul: the anonymous giants of our traditional liturgy, the great
poets of Spain: Yehudah HaLevi, Avraham Ibn Ezra; the kabbalist-
innovators of Safed – Shlomo HaLevi Alqabetz, the Ari, Avraham
Maimin, Eleazar Azikri; the Ḥasidic Masters – the Ba'al Shem Tov,

Levi Yitzḥak of Berditchev, Aaron the Great of Karlin; and then his own rebbes – Rabbi Joseph Isaac Schneersohn and his successor, the late Rabbi Menaḥem Mendel Schneersohn.

But it is more. As the material for this anthology grew, and as old translations were dug out of the archives and brushed off, it became clearer to me than ever before that this *rebbe* is a master—a master of the word, a master of the letter, a master of the song, a master of the rhyme and the rhythm, a master of the *niggun*, a master of music, a master of intercession, and above all, a master of prayer. For after all, when the last note fades away from off the surface of the ear drum, and the last letter disappears from the eye's retina, there only remains one thing of importance: I and Thou. For this is his purpose, for this his soul yearns: to come into the garden of the beloved and for the beloved to dwell within.

And this is the secret of this little book.

It is not just a compilation of translated *Sacred Verse* interposed with original compositions; it is really a gateway into the *Sacred Soul* and, as we have learned, the soul has five levels starting from the body-soul stretching 'back' through the dimensions where the souls begin to merge, yours and mine, until they reach the Source. And Reb Zalman brings us the tools for this sacred Journey: that of *holy* laughter and *holy* ḥutzpah: that of *holy* music and *holy* dance; that of *holy* tears and *holy* cries; that of *holy* sounds and *holy* letters; that of *holy* t'shuvah (repentance) and that of *holy* friendship. Through these poems we can hear all the voices and see all the faces of the *rebbe*.

As I worked on editing the personal introductions, I could hear his voice and feel his smile, and I could enter his life, his mind, and his heart and appreciate the incredible gifts that he has been endowed with, and which he so much wishes to share with us. Look at the genius with which he is able to replicate acrostics (letter formations from the first letter of each verse) both in Hebrew and in English, whether it is the name of the composer, or the English Alphabet or the Hebrew *Aleph-Bet*. And not only are these translations that preserve the meaning and acrostic of the original, but miraculously Reb Zalman manages to preserve the timbre so that, as we have so often done, the original and the translation can be sung together in perfect synchronicity.

And then there are Reb Zalman's own creations where we hear him cry out—*Abba, Abba* (Father, Father) (p. 93), or mourn the passing of his *rebbe* (p. 148), or cry out for a Divine kiss (p. 159), or praise the courage of Allen Ginsberg (p. 150), a fellow trailblazer.

And as if this were not enough, we are told of the melodies that he either composed or adapted to accompany many of these creations. These can be heard in the master's voice on the website dedicated to this book www.gaonbooks.com/AllBreathingLife.

Finally, I would like to thank Reb Reuven Goldfarb for his meticulous reading and editing of the finer points of poetry that elude me. Only a poet such as Reuven—with a sensitivity not only to the word in general, but to Reb Zalman's word in particular— could have accomplished this. To my soul friend Netanel Miles-Yepez - blessed be your hawk eyes and sensitive spirit. And lastly, I wish to thank Reb Zalman himself for entrusting me with this part of his Torah so that it has become integrated into my Torah and hopefully into your Torah.

Dr. Michael Kagan
Jerusalem, 2011

At The Interface Between Poetry And Prayer

Introduction
Jewish Sacred Poetry

Why Do I Want to Share This?

I remember how dismayed I was whenever I saw an anthology of spiritual writings in which there was a lot of material from Hindu, Sufi, and Christian spiritual writers, and in vain did I look for Jewish writings that would show heart, soul, and spirit. I knew well that they existed, but alas, only in their Hebrew originals. I was also aware of the fact that many of the editors of Jewish prayer manuals often translated or rendered the original liturgical material to be read by the discursive mind. However, the original Hebrew was never meant to be scanned silently with the eyes alone. There is something about sacred poetry that demands chanting in such a way that the words will arouse feelings in the heart of the worshiper.

While Martin Buber, in his amazing and powerful work *I and Thou*, made it clear that in the immediacy of the human-Divine encounter we were not dealing with objects, and thereby brought us into the sense of the dialogue, there was little understanding on the part of his readers of the right brain and left brain difference.

If I were to speak of this from the point of view of the Kabbalah and the Four Worlds[1], the people who worked in Jewish scholarship – *Judische Wissenschaft*[2] – were all dedicated to showing how Judaism was a "religion of reason," in the Kantian sense; and even if they did touch poetry, it was only for the sake of analyzing it to be at the service of the rational mind. They only operated in the world of

[1]   The four worlds are: *Assiya* (action), *Yetzira* (formation), *B'riya* (creation), and *Atzilut* (emanation) which correspond to: body, heart, mind and spirit.

[2]   'Jewish Science,' the German name for the historical—critical school that arose in the first half of the 19th century.

Assiya (deed), dealing with grammar and history, or with the world of *B'riya* (intellect) with the concepts touched by the poetry.

A poet does not write in order to present the linguist or art historian with a word-cadaver to dissect and catalog. The poets, possessed by the *Daemon*, the devotional Muse, find themselves captivated by enchantment, and such enchantment they wish to share with others. The poet is attuned to an imaginal reality that exists in a world of its own. The reader can choose not to enter into the world of the parable, the *Olam HaMashal,* but, as Kafka pointed out, all he has then gained is entrance into the world of things.

Spiritual poetry is a launching platform to take the person who will lovingly recite it into another realm. Those of us who are acquainted with the second part of the daily Hebrew prayer service known as *P'sukei de-Zimrah*[3] and have been able to enter into it have learned to give thanks for the privilege of joining King David and the Levites in the Temple in the *Yishtabah* prayer. (page 27) The lover of God wants to express his or her longing for intimacy with the Beloved with the sounds of *niggunim*[4], and the words that accompany them. The more they can enter into the reality behind the words, the closer they will feel to the Divine Presence.

While sensation deals with things, and reason with concepts and ideas, neither is in the dialogical position. The one who wants to face the living God—in the *Shiviti*[5]—needs to do it with the heart. However, the heart needs an Other; it needs to be in relationship. In this way, sacred poetry becomes a password to a tryst with the Beloved, bringing one closer to facing the Divine Other. (Even if philosophical reason is anchored in an absolute monism in which there is no Other, the heart must nevertheless set reason aside in order to encounter the Beloved.

---

3   'Verses of praise' which corresponds to the second world of emotions.

4   'Melody' or 'tune.' The Ḥasidic movement views the melody as one of the gates through which to enter to the Divine Presence.

5   *Shiviti* is the first word in verse 8 of Psalm 16: "*I have set the Divine before me always.*" In this context it is understood to be the Holy Embrace, face-to-face as the *K'ruvim* in the Holy of Holies.

In my poem, "The Prayer of a Monist" (p. 155), I made an attempt in my poem to satisfy both heart and mind.)

What Were My Motives?

As I said, very seldom were we able to find translations of hymns and prayers that spoke to the heart. In Great Britain, in the Victorian era, there were some beautiful translations made that echoed the language of the Anglican *Book of Common Prayer.* The early American Reform Movement did likewise in its hymnal. There were times when I would joyfully sing: "*Come O Sabbath day and bring—peace and healing on thy wing—and to every troubled breast—speak of the divine behest—thou shalt rest, thou shalt rest.*" It had the power to move me emotionally, as did: "*At the Dawn I seek Thee—Refuge, Rock Divine.*" Perhaps it was my Hapsburg origins, but I found that I was alone; others did not feel the same way. The language was too stilted, the imagery too archaic. The God we want to encounter is not so regally formal. Isn't it incongruous to want to be hugged by the sovereign deity in front of all the Angels and heavenly saints? Contrast this to when we enter the Divine Presence through the eroticism of the Song of Songs saying: "*Kiss me with the kisses of your mouth; your loving is more intoxicating than wine.*" Once having discovered those precious moments of elation in the tryst with God in one's heart, one can no longer be satisfied with the formality of the Victorian English. So how could I render the feelings of longing and closeness that I felt as I recited the Hebrew devotional love poems?

It is for this reason that I first felt the very strong need to translate *Yedid Nefesh*[6] of Eleazar Azikri[7]. Similarly, I found the usual translations of the *An'im Z'mirot*[8] stodgy and lacking the devotional intent that the Ḥasidei Ashkenaz[9] originally imbued it with.

6   *You Who Love My Soul,* Page 79
7   R' Eleazar Azikri was a Safed kabbalist (1533-1600)
8   *A Hymn of Glory,* Page 30
9   The Ḥasidei Ashkenaz (literally "the Pious of Germany") was a Jewish movement in the 12th and 13th century, founded by Rabbi Judah the

I was mostly guided by introspection to the feelings of fervor I experienced in prayer, in reciting the Psalms and in chanting the poetry. So when I veered from the literal denotative meaning of some of the words, and allowed myself the freedom to express those connotations implied within the original Hebrew words, I felt that I had the right to place them on the page in that way.

Aesthetics have a way of changing with the changing culture. One only needs to listen to the popular songs of this generation to recognize what language would allow the generation to feel sacred enchantment.

I cannot possibly name all the people with whom I shared these materials and who helped me to refine them. The numerous weekend retreats and workshops, High Holy Day services; all of these were vessels in which these poem-prayers matured, allowing them to take on the deep flavor of the many souls who prayed them, sang them, and cried tears through them.

And how could I not be overflowing with thanks to Michael Kagan for his continued interest in bringing these efforts to a larger audience? I'm grateful to God that I had the privilege of sharing with him and his wife Rabbi Ruth Gan Kagan. They have become the vital connectors for Israelis to Jewish renewal.

And to my student, friend, ḥevruta, apprentice, teacher, Netanel Miles-Yepez, who sits so well-balanced on the three-fold fence, and without whom so much would not be done – my eternal thanks.

Pious of Regensburg, Germany.

I

From the Order of the Prayers

Nishmat
All Breathing Life Adores Your Name

There are times when I feel that I need no other prayer than the *Nishmat*. I prefer to take my time with it. I take each phrase, tasting it as I pronounce it, and then spend time in my imagination bringing it to life in a loving way so that I feel it in my heart. To enter into the prayer of *Nishmat* is to enter the enchantment of the miraculous order. Try reading it slowly and out loud so that you can hear and stress the sense of the second person, the I facing the Thou, addressing the God in whose presence you are.

All breathing life
adores Your Name;
Yah, our God -
All flesh alive
is raised to ecstasy
each time we become aware of You!
Beyond endless Time and Space that's vast
You are Divine.
Only You are the One who
ultimately extricates and frees,
ransoms, saves and sustains us
and cares when we are in distress;
You, You alone secure our lives.

You, ultimate Cause and ultimate Effect,
Source of all Creation;
You manifest in all birthing.
In every compliment it is You we praise
You manage Your universe with kindness -
with compassion all beings in it.

Yah ever awake and ever alert!
You rouse us from the deepest sleep

You give words to the speechless
You release the imprisoned
You support the stumbling
You give dignity to the downtrodden
Every appreciation we offer is Yours.

If ocean-full our mouth were with music
Our tongues singing like the ceaseless surf
Our lips praising You to the skies
Our eyes blazing like sun and moon
Our arms spread like soaring eagles
Our legs sprinting like those of deer
We could not thank You enough
Yah! Our God, our parents' God!
Neither could we celebrate by naming
the times exceeding millions
the places exceeding billions
the favors You did
for our parents and for us.

Yah! Oh God!
From oppression You redeemed us,
Now we can never be at home in slavery -
During famines You fed us enough
to live on
You shielded us from wars and plagues,
From diseases of body and mind
you pulled us out.
To this moment Your caring helped us,
We never lacked Your kindness –
Please don't ever abandon us God!
Our limbs each want to thank you,
The air of each breath You breathed into us,
Their very substance bless with gratitude
with praise and celebration
honoring that exalted holiness
so majestic, that is Your fame!
Our speech is appreciation
Our expression an oath of loyalty

Our attitude surrender
Our stance before You obedience
Our feelings overwhelming awe
Our inners singing scales of Your Names
As it is in Scripture:
All my very essence exclaims:
Yah! Who? Like You?
You inspire the gentle to stand up to the bully,
The poor disempowered to stand up to the thug.

No other can claim to be what You are
No other can pretend to be
THE GREAT GOD
THE MIGHTY, THE AWESOME,
THE GOD, MOST HIGH
Yet nesting in Heavens and Earth!
So we will keep celebrating and delighting
and blessing Your Holy Name with David:
"Yahhh! breathes my soul out to You.
All my inners pulse with You!"

Potent God Force!
Magnanimous in Glory,
Ever prevailing,
Awesome Mystery!
Majestic One, who presides over all destiny!
Eternal *Sh'khinah*, Holy Beyond,
Saints sing Yah!
In harmony with decent folks.

Good people exalt You,
Saints are Your blessing,
Devotees sanctify You,
You delight in our inner holiness.

Y'hi Kh'vod
Yah! Fill our World to Reflect Your Nobility

This prayer is the epitome of what is to come after-wards. On the occasions when I must rush and cannot say the rest of the Psalms, I still will say this one here. It has the power to bring us the realization that each moment is sustained by the living God. Embrace these words and make them their own.

Yah! Fill our world to reflect Your nobility
So You will find joy in Your creation.

We adore Your name ever,
In all circumstances.

Those who come from the East
And those who come from the West
Celebrate Your Name in their ways.
Yah transcends all national bigotries
Her glory is in what concerns Heaven.

Yah – this is Your Name forever
Yah is the watchword
Each generation passes to the next.

Yah! You have set Your Sh'khinah in the Heavens
Your domain encompasses all there is.

So Heaven is glad
Earth is happy
All nations agree that
You are in charge.

Yah! You are now
Yah! You were then

Yah! You will be
Constant for ever.
Yah! Your reign is eternal
Earth is Yours alone
No nation can claim her.

You Yah void the designs of tyrants
You Yah block their schemes.

People brood over so many desires
It is Your design Yah that prevails.

What You Yah design
Lasts through all time;
What You propose
Works for many generations.

You speak and it becomes real
You command and it comes to existence.

You Yah chose Zion
You wish to make Your seat there.

You Yah have singled out Jacob
Israel is Your treasure.

You Yah will not desert Your people
You will not forsake Your heritage.

Because You are caring
You will forgive sin
You will not destroy
But time and again
You will subdue Your wrath
And not let Your fury rise.

Yah! Please help,
Prince!
Answer us the same day
When we cry out.

Yishtabaḥ
Your Name be Praised

One day I was so enjoying some classical music that I decided to "beam it" to God to enjoy with me, to taste my delight. I offered it to God like a holy sacrifice, a raising-up of my delight, as if to say, "Hear God, taste what it is for this human being to enjoy the rhythm and the harmony and the flight of sacred feelings." It was then that I allowed myself to translate the running synonyms of Hebrew terms in this prayer into the words of musical notation. Allow yourself as you recite this prayer to bring back into your awareness some Aria, a movement of a Symphony, or a particularly touching song. See what it feels like to open your awareness and invite the presence of God to enjoy the music with you.

Your Name be praised, always
Majestic One.
Powerful and gentle Source,
Making Heaven and Earth sacred.
It is our pleasure to dedicate to You,
Our God and Our parents' God,
Time and again:
Music and Celebration,
Jubilation and Symphony,
Fortissimo, Anthem,
Victory March, Largo Forte,
Paean and Hymn,
Sanctus and Maestoso,
Laudo and Aria,
Celebrating Your Divine reputation
In every realm.

We worship You, Yah,
Generous, Great, Regal One
Who is the One
To whom we offer all these.

God whom we appreciate,
Source of all wonder,
Fountain of all souls,
Author of all that happens.

Yequm Purqan
From Heaven Let our Freedom Flow

This prayer, originally written in Aramaic, asks God's help for the students of Torah. I first heard it sung in Yiddish. I do not know who composed the melody and shaped the Yiddish words based on the prayer. I do know that when there was a great meeting in 1936 in Vienna of the Agudat Yisrael[10] this song made its appearance.

> From Heaven let our freedom flow
> Favor Mercy and kindness show
> Ample life years, ample living
> With God's helpful blessing glow.
>
> Generations well and strong
> Generations that belong
> To God's *Mitzvot* and the Torah
> Engaging in them all life long.
>
> Teachers, Rabbis, Ḥavurot
> Learning Torah – polyglot
> Heads of *Yeshivot*, magistrates
> And their students, all Torah gates.
>
> Everyone who spends their time
> Even studying just one line
> May God's blessings fill their life
> And save them all from war and strife.

---

10   Agudat Yisrael was founded in Katowice (Upper Silesia, now in the southwestern part of Poland), in 1912, with purpose of providing an umbrella organization for observant Jews who opposed the Zionist movement.

An'im Z'mirot
A Hymn Of Glory

Having had the opportunity of observing the chanting of Christian monks, people who preserved medieval traditions, I have the sense that this very beautiful and holy prayer deserves this kind of reenactment in the form of a responsive chant by seriously devout people. (It is a pity that in many synagogues this sacred poem is given to the children to rush through at the end of the Shabbat service.) Find a friend, and then facing one another, start the chant. Take it slowly and devotionally, reciprocating every two lines, taking a pause of at least one breath for reflection before you respond. When completed, share with each other what insights this experience has brought you.

I chant to please You, I weave You dear songs
For You my soul yearns, For You she longs.
Nestled in Your palm, her love for You grows
She will not rest until it's You she knows!
I look for words to speak Your praises
My heart to You its yearning raises.
Therefore I will speak the virtues of Your Fame
And garland with excellence the honor of Your Name.
Though I do not see You, still I draw Your Face
Portray Your features, name Your Place.
Your prophets spoke, Your servants darkly knew
In symbols and myths they referred to You.
When describing your pow'r and declaring Your care
Of Your awesome compassion they made us aware.
Yet it is not Your Being that they could describe
Only the way Your compassion's Your vibe.
Countless their visions of Your mysterious feats
In all their forms Your ONEness meets.
They saw You young, they saw You old
They saw You patient, They saw You bold.

Ancient of Days Eternally just
Each moment our Helper in Whom we trust.
Wearing Your helmet as hero to help us
Your strong arm, Your right hand to save us.
Your hair drenched with light drops, all shining with brilliance.
Your Darkness is shelter, Your love in all radiance.
How fair is Your kindness, how splendid Your sight
May our song rise to crown You with endearing delight
A jewel all golden Your image sends rays
with t'fillin on forehead we follow Your ways.
With grace and honor, all splendid in glory
Your people sing loudly Your triumphal story
In words of young lovers they gaze at Your visage
the letters of Torah in black hold Your message.
Justice Your mantle in balance with kindness
This gives You pleasure, delight and sublimeness.
May we deserve to be scepter in Your regal hand
A crimson royal cape, we Your loyal band.
The burdened sufferers, You sustained them with might
How precious You held them, so dear to Your sight.
Your glory my pride is, my delight for Your care
So close You are, to answer my pray'r.
Your shining face illumines my days
I am awed by the magic revealed in Your ways.
To Moshe You showed Your Head-T'fillin's knot
Your image was clear in his mind and his thought.
Though humble Your folk, they are Your proud fame
You're enthroned on their praises, they honor Your Name.
Truth is Your Word, enduring its worth
From parent to child its message flows forth.
I cannot sing your praises complete,
May those that I do sing and reach You be sweet.
Like perfume and incense may my singing rise high
A paean to crown You, a poor lover's sigh.
My poor song devoid is of all artifice
Still this loving song is my best sacrifice.
My blessings are lifting to rise to new heights,
To make fertile the birth of the Tzaddik with might.

And with these blessings, these love words so fond.
With a nod of Your head, I ask You: Respond.
Regard please these poor words that I blush to recite
My soul's ardent longing to give You delight.

Adon Olam
You were Cosmic Lord

I remember some melodies that were used to sing this poetic hymn to God in Europe before the Holocaust, especially the one that was used for the High Holy Days, that does more justice to the content than any of the contemporary tunes popular today. This beautiful hymn still awaits a composer who will write an anthem grand and subtle enough to contain these words.

You were cosmic Lord *Adonay Malakh*
Before there even was a world
Then Your will all things did make
Adonay Melekh we call you now.

And when all things will cease to be
Adonay Yimlokh still true will be
You were, You are, eternally
Resplendent to infinity.

You alone, there are not two
To join as friends, as lovers do.
Beginningless and without end
You keep all one by plan and strength.

You are my God, Redeemer true,
Protecting me in war, in strife.
My holy haven and my flag
My cup of health for what I lack.

Into Your hand I trust my breath
You breathe in me by night by day
My body is your tool, your gift,
With you as mine I am not afraid.

Ahavat Olam
Everlasting Love

In some prayer books, instead of using the expression *ahavat olam*, meaning 'everlasting love', they use the words *ahavah rabbah*, meaning 'great, immense love'. In the mystical writings, much is written about the distinction. It occurs to me that when men feel the fervor of their love, they speak of its immensity. When women speak of the love they desire, they want it to be enduring forever. Not long ago, I heard an interview with a seasoned clergyman: When he was asked what his prayer life was about these days, he answered that he just makes himself present to be loved by God. I believe that this prayer invites us to do just that. While reciting it, find a place to pause and make yourself present to be loved by God.

From ever
You have loved us into life.
Yah, our God –
You nourished us with kindness
and abundance.

Holy One!
For the sake of Your plan,
for Your honor,
and because we know
that our parents trusted You,
and You, in turn, taught them
how to live life
so as to be serving Your purpose.
We ask You to share with us
in the same way.
God, kind Parent,
we live in the embrace
of Your caring.
Make ours an understanding heart,

to become aware and
be careful and effective,
in this way to make real
what You speak to us in Torah
and with so much love.

When we study Torah,
may we see clearly
what is meant for us to know.
When we do *Mitzvot* (Divine Instructions),
may all our feelings
sit harmoniously in our hearts.

Focus all our hearts' longing
to that moment
when we stand in Your Presence
in both awe and adoration.

May we never have to be apologetic
for our love for You.

Trusting You,
we are happy to see
your beneficent plan unfolding.

May Your kindness and compassion
be available to us.
Please hurry,
bring blessing and peace to us.
Gather us, so we not be scattered
all over the world.
Lift the hold of estrangement from us.
Lead us to live in this world
so that we feel at home in it.

You can do this for us.
You have assigned us
to do our special work in life

You brought us close to You.
We are grateful.
We hold You special
and are filled with love for You,
You are Blessed, Yah,
who relates to us in Love.
Amen.

Sh'ma'
Listen and Hear

This version of the translation of the *Sh'ma'* is not the one we're used to in the usual translations that are made from the biblical source in Deuteronomy. Most people have not learned to enter the metaphor in a way that makes them find something helpful for the way in which we live our everyday lives. When teaching the *Sh'ma'* I suggest to people that they recite it four or five times with the following intention: the first time, substituting one's own name for the word 'Yisrael.' The second time, putting the name of a person with whom one would want to share this moment of unification with God to the word 'Yisrael.'. The third time, intending that as we recite the *Sh'ma'* we deposit this moment of awareness so that it will come back to us at moment of our dying. The fourth time, to say it as if Moses, our teacher were addressing us. The fifth time, to hold all these intentions simultaneously.

Listen you *Yisrael* person,
(say your own name here)
Yah who Is, is our God,
Yah who Is,
is One, Unique, All there Is.

Through time and space
Your glory shines, Majestic One.

Love Yah, who is your God,
in what your heart is,
in what you aspire to,
in what you have made your own.
May these values
which I connect with your life
be implanted in your feelings.
May they become the norm

for your children:
address them
in the privacy of your home,
and on the errands you run.
May they help you relax
and activate you to be productive.
Display them visibly on your arm.
Let them focus your attention.
See them at all transitions at home
and in your environment.

How good it will be
when you really listen
and hear my directions
which I give to you today
for loving Yah who is your God
and to act godly
with feeling and inspiration.
Your earthly needs will be met
at the right time,
appropriate to the season.
You will reap what you planted
for your delight and health.
Also your animals will have ample feed.
All of you will eat and be content.

Be careful – watch out!
Don't let your cravings delude you;
don't become alienated;
don't let your cravings
become your gods;
don't debase yourself to them
because the God-sense within you
will become distorted.
Heaven will be shut to you,
grace will not descend,
Earth will not yield her produce.
Your rushing will destroy you!

And Earth will not be able
to recover her good balance
in which God's gifts manifest.

May these values of Mine reside
in your feelings and aspirations:
marking what you produce,
guiding what you perceive.
Teach them to your children
so that they are instructed
how to make their homes sacred
and how they deal with traffic.
(May these values of Mine reside
in your feelings and aspirations)
even when you are depressed
and when you are elated.
Mark your entrances and exits
with them,
so you will be more aware.
Then, you and your children
and their children,
will live out on earth
that divine promise
given to your ancestors
to live heavenly days
right here on this earth.

Yah Who Is, said to Moses,
"Speak, telling the Israel folks
to make *tzitzit* (tassels)
on the corners of their garments,
so they will have generations
to follow them.
On each *tzitzit* let them set
a blue thread.
These *tzitzit* are for your benefit!
Glance at them,
and in your seeing remember

all the other directives of Yah Who Is,
and act on them!
This way you will not be led astray,
craving to see and want
and then prostitute yourself
for your cravings.
This way you will be mindful
to actualize my directions
for becoming dedicated to your God;
to be aware that
I Am Yah Who is your God,
Who is the One who freed you
from oppression
in order to God you.
I am Yah who is your God."

Ana b'Khoaḥ
Strengthen Us

I like to chant *Ana b'Khoaḥ*[11] –Strengthen Us – using the melody that comes to us from the Rhizhiner Rebbe,[12] which includes his sighs known as *Dem Rhizhiner's Krekhts*. It is considered by many to be a very potent passkey that takes our prayers directly to God, even when other avenues are blocked. It has been my custom to recite it whenever I hear a siren – be it of a police cruiser, an ambulance, fire truck – as an "arrow prayer" – that they might come in time to save lives. It is good to use it as a concluding prayer to personal petitioning.

Source of Mercy,
With loving strength,
Untie our tangles.

Your chanting folk,
Raise high, make pure,
Accept our song.

Like Your own eye,
Lord keep us safe,
Who union seek with You.

Cleanse and bless us,
Infuse us ever
With loving care.

Gracious source
Of holy power!

11   Traditionally attributed to the first century Rabbi Neḥunia ben Haqqaneh.
12   Rebbe Yisrael of Ruzhin (d. 5611 [1751]), commonly known as the Holy Rizhiner, was the great-grandson of the Maggid of Mezritch.

Do guide your folk.
Sublime and holy One,
Do turn to us,
Of holy chant.

Receive our prayer,
Do hear our cry,
Who secrets knows.

Through time and space
Your glory shines,
Majestic One.

Pataḥ Eliyahu
Elijah Began Saying

In many Hasidic and kabbalistic prayer books, this chapter from the opening of the *Tikuney Zohar*[13] is suggested to the worshiper as a preparation for worship. The splendid vista of the kabbalistic cosmological panorama[14] unfolds in it, tempting one away from the infantilized version of an anthropomorphic God. What is so remarkable is that Prophet Elijah, in teaching us about God, does not speak about God in the third person. It would be a disregard of the presence of God to speak as if God were absent. Therefore, he addresses God about God and allows us to listen-in. Often, while reciting this, I find myself captivated by a particular phrase that demands I enter into a contemplative state, holding the moment. Give yourself permission and time to let this happen to you, too.

Elijah began saying:
Lord of the worlds
You Who are One
and not just a number
You are the highest
of the highest
most hidden
of the undisclosed
no thought scheme
grasps You
at all.

---

13   *Tikuney HaZohar* (or *Tikkunim* - Adornments) contains seventy discourses on the first word of the Torah - *Beraisheet*
14   The term *S'firot* refers to the ten emanations of the Divine from the most infinite to the most immanent.

You are He
Who pours forth
Ten *Tikkunim*.
We call them
the Ten *S'firot*,
lead through them
Worlds hidden and undisclosed
and Worlds manifest and known.

In them are You hidden
from the sons of men.
You are He
Who binds them,
Who unites them.

And since You are
within them
whosoever
sunders
one from its mate
of these Ten *S'firot*
to him it is accounted
as if he had
sundered You.

These Ten *S'firot*
proceed in their order
one—long
one—short
and one between.

You are the One
who governs them.
No one
governs You
neither below
nor above
nor at any side.

You made wraps for them
(the Ten S'firot)
from whence blossom forth
souls
for the sons of men.

Many bodies You fashioned
for them
"bodies" they are called
when compared to the "wraps"
covering them.

They are thus called
in the following Tikkun:

Ḥesed	the "Right Arm"
Gevurah	the "Left Arm"
Tiferet	the "Trunk"
Netzaḥ & Hod	the two "Thighs"
Y'sod	the trunk's "Extremity"; sign of the Covenant most holy
Malkhut	the "Orifice"; the oral Torah we call it
Hokhmah	the "Brain"; it is the Thought within
Binah	the "Heart" in it understands the very heart of understanding

Concerning these two
(Hokhmah and Binah)
it is written
"Mysteries hidden
are they of YHVH God"

Keter, the highest,
for it is
the Crown of Majesty,
concerning it is said:
He tells the End
from the Beginning.

It is the scalp
of the *t'fillin*;
within
it is the '*Mah*' name
(of value 45)

YUD-HA-VAV-HA
it is the Heaven-way of
Atzilut – Emanation.
The rooting place of the Tree
of Boughs and Branches.
Like water
drenching the Tree
causing it to increase
through the root's sap.

O Lord of the worlds
You are
Origin of Origins
Cause of Causes
Who drenches
that Tree
by this flux.
And this flux
like soul to body
is the body's life.

In You
there is nothing
like image
or form
of anything
within or without.
You create
Heaven and Earth
bringing forth
of their substance
Sun, Moon

Planets, Stars.
And on Earth,
grass and trees
a Garden of Eden
flora and fauna
beasts, birds, fish
and Man.

All this so that
what is above
may become known
so that we may have
models
of those above and below.
Those above can become known
through those below
(and since there is no model
in creation for You)
there is no one who knows
You at all.

Outside of You
there is no One
(whole—all—complete)
among those above
and those below –
Thus are You made known
as the Origin of All
and the Master of All.

Each S'firah,
has a known Name
by these Names
Angels are called.
(An Angel –
entity of force
directed to an aim,
an energy discharged

by its own function.)
You have no known Name
because all the Names
are filled by You.
You are the fulfillment
of them all.
When You rise up from them
all the Names remain
as bodies bereft of soul.

You are wise
yet not in wisdom known
You are understanding
yet not in understanding known
In You there is no place for knowledge
(to hold on).

But Your power and strength
You make knowable to Man
as You show to him
how the world
is conducted
in Law and Mercy
For there is Righteousness and Justice
according to the deeds
of the sons of Man.

Law is *Gevurah*
Justice – the middle column
Righteousness – the Holy Majesty
the just scales
two true supports
the righteous HIN
(liquid measure) –
is the Holy Covenant.

All this portrays
how the world is conducted

but not that there is
in You
known righteousness
identical with Law
(which binds You)
Nor is there Justice in You
which is Mercy
or any other attribute at all.

Be drawn down to us
– Blessed channeled
YHVH
into the world
for ever
truly so truly so
Amen Amen.

K'gavna
Just as They...

This sublime passage, taken from the Zohar and recited by Ḥasidim in the middle of the Friday night prayer service, describes the moment of entering the Shabbat in our world in terms of the Shabbat in the heavenly realms. It is filled with mystical references that require prolonged and deep study, but I have found that simply chanting these secrets opens up for me the mysteries of Shabbat.

Just as they
Ḥesed, G'vurah, and Tiferet,
Netzaḥ, Hod,
and Y'sod on high
become One mind and One purpose
so does She,
Malkhut here below
unite in the mystery of Oneness
to be at One with those above
to receive the Holy One, blessed be He.
The holy One, blessed be He,
does not seat Himself
on His glorious throne,
until She, the Shekhina
turns to the mystery of Oneness
as He does
in order that One and One
would become One.
This is the mystery
of "Yah is One
and God's Name is One."
The mystery of the Sabbath
is the Sabbath Herself.
It is Her uniting
with the secret of Oneness,

of uniqueness,
that She may immerse
in the Secret of One.
The prayer of the ascent of the Sabbath
is the holding on
to the glorious holy throne
in the secret of Oneness.
As she, the Sabbath,
enters into union
She sheds the side of otherness
and all judgment and harshness
pass from Her
and She remains in union
with the holy radiance
and crowns Herself
with many crowns
as she faces the Holy King.
All holders of wrathful power,
all relentless condemners,
are totally confused and pass from Her
and in the whole universe
there are no sovereign others
beside Her.
Her face shines with a sublime radiance,
as She is crowned below
by the holy people
who themselves all become
enwrapped and crowned
with new supernal souls
in order that the service of worship
be a blissful one,.
to praise Her in Joy
with radiant faces
to say "We Bless You."

Taḥanun
A Supplication

Unfortunately, much of what we find in the penitential liturgy makes us sound like nebbish wimps. We portray ourselves as being victims and complain about how much we are suffering and try to cajole God to forgive us because we suffer. What is really important is that *Taḥanun* (supplication) should be a moment in which we get into the process of *t'shuvah* (repentance). Mere reciting of these sentences, a practice that may have been more appropriate in the past than in the present, doesn't seem to help us. The best thing would be to enter into a silence, to remember a flaw in our behavior or our character, to hold it up to God and to ask for help to be able to correct that flaw. Out of the silence there are times when we become aware of a response. It is good to remember what comes to us in such moments, and even to make notes so that we can work on it later.

My God!
My soul is Yours,
my body is Your servant,
take pity on what You have created.
My soul is Yours
and my body is Yours,
God help us for Your sake.
We come to You
because we want to honor
Your reputation.
Help us in our moral struggle
for the sake of Your reputation
because You are kind and compassionate.
Forgive us,
for there is so much
we need to be forgiven for.
Pardon us our Father,

our errors are so great.
Forgive us our Royal Master,
many are our mistakes.
Our God, our parents' God,
pardon our sins,
erase our rebellions,
let our failures not appear before You.
Mold our drives to serve Your purposes;
let our stubbornness be in Your service.
Refresh our conscience
to guard Your instructions;
Sensitize our hearts to love You
and to respect Your reputation
as Your Torah prescribes:
"and YaH Your God
will sensitize Your heart
and the hearts of Your children
so that Your love for Your God
will be wholehearted, inspired,
to make Your life meaningful."
Dear God,
I approach You
from the desire to serve You
and yet there is no *Tzaddik*
who can do only good
and not fail and fall.
Please help me with my moral life
so that in every way
my attitude will be balanced
and right.
To begin with,
help me to forgive anyone
who has frustrated and upset me;
whether they have sinned against me,
my body, my possessions,
my reputation, anything of mine;
whether unintentionally or intentionally;
whether they schemed to do it

or were unaware;
whether it was in word or action;
whether is was in thought
or in the imagination;
whether it was in this incarnation
or in any other:
I completely forgive any God-wrestler;
and let no one be punished on my account.
My God and my parents God,
may our prayer come before You;
do not turn Your attention
from our pleading.
We don't want to be impudent,
we don't want to be stubborn
and claim that we are righteous
and have not sinned.
Indeed our parents have sinned
and we have sinned.

Help us God, not to fail You again.
And what I have done wrong
or failed to do right,
I hereby confess to You.

I beg You,
that in Your great mercy
You erase my sins,
but not by means
of suffering and illness.
May the words of my mouth and the meditation of my heart
be acceptable for You, Yah, my Rock and my Redeemer.
I place my faith in You,
I place my trust in You,
I place my hope in You.

Aleynu
We Rise to Praise You

People were so taken by the message of this Aleynu prayer recited on Rosh Hashannah, that they co-opted it as the finale of all the daily prayers. However, there is a phrase that was not originally complementary to people who follow other religions: "for they bow down to emptiness and void, while we bow down to the King of Kings, the Holy One, blessed be He." In 1975, I needed a prayer quorum to help me during the mourning (*Shiv'ah*) week for my father of blessed memory. I was then in Boulder, Colorado, as I am now, teaching at the newly founded Naropa Institute where there were a considerable number of Jewish Buddhists. A quorum was formed with these Jews, but when I came to the words "they bow down to emptiness and the void" these words took on an entirely different meaning, pointing to the Buddhist awareness of *Shunyata*, the awareness that all things are 'void' of inherent existence.

We rise to praise, You Source of All,
Your generous work as Creator of All.
You made us one with all of Life.
You helped us to share with all mankind.
You linked our fate with all that lives
and made our portion
with all in the world.

Some of us like to worship You as emptiness and void;
Some of us want to worship You as King of Kings;
We all consider You sacred and blessed.
We stand amazed at the vault of the sky,
At the firmness of Earth,
And deem You enthroned
in the Highest realms,
dwelling also in and with us.

You are our God –
there is nothing else.
Your Truth is supreme.
Existence is nothing but You,
so Your Torah guides us.
Yah's kingdom extends
throughout the Cosmos.
Further it is stated:
Yah will indeed govern over all there is.
On that Day, Yah will be One
and Her Name will be ONE.

II

Songs of the Holy Shabbat

Shabbat Refrain I

Every Friday evening people come together using the standard Hebrew Psalms and hymns to joyously welcome in the Shabbat. Once when I had to lead a congregation in this prayer service, I felt the need for adding something extra that could be sung in order to increase the special awareness of Shabbat. So I composed the following, setting it to a melody that originally came from Chabad Hasidism and was used as the melody for a sweet lullaby.

Another week is now completed
And the Shabbos is its goal
Our very spirits that have been depleted
Receive on Shabbos a supernal soul
And if our hopes seem all defeated
The victor on Shabbos is the soul.

Life and its struggle like waves of storm
Engulf the island of our peace
But on Shabbos we find our norm
And all the tensions and sorrows cease
A holy mood fills our fleshly form
Earthly woes all find surcease.

Thus on Shabbos we sate the yearning
For God's wisdom, love and will
We are imbued with the Torah's learning
Into our natures it to instill
To worlds yet coming we will be turning
And God's law we will fulfill.

Shabbat Refrain II

There is a special atmosphere that descends as everyone prepares for Shabbat, as we gather to enter into that holy precinct in time. To give expression to these feelings, I wrote the following song and composed a melody[15] which can act as a sort of virtual *mikveh*, immersion of purification, for the consciousness, as a prelude for the complete immersion of mind, body, and soul in the approaching rendezvous with the beloved Shabbat itself.

Shabbos peace and Shabbos blessing
Enter Holy Presence Now
Bring new *Neshamah* soul's progression
Remove the week's sweat from my brow.

Heaven, earth, and all between them
Can on this day be at rest
Just a little while before this
God's *tov me'od* declared you best.

As God planned in Yah's creation
We for God a place shall make
Royal priests, O holy nation,
To this service some awake.

Body, mind and heart and spirit
No longer turn away from Him
Shabbos rhythm of the *Sh'khinah*
Makes for peace without, within.
Being is the state of Shabbos

---

15   Recorded in the CD "Prelude for a Rendezvous with the Beloved". Note that the first letter of each verse spells out the world SHABBOS (Sabbath). *Neshamah* is a level of the soul; *Tov-Me'od* means very good said after the completion of the Creation; *Sh'khinah* is the immanent spirit of the Divine; *Mishpakhah* is the family; *Olam Haba* is the world to come.

We left doing to the week
Breathing deeper, gone are burdens
We have found and need not seek.

Our beloved here together
Let us bless each other's seeds
Let us nourish, feed each other
Gaining respite from our needs.

Sh'khinah's children, sentient beings
Sister, brother *Mishpakhah*
Celebrate Messiah vision
Shabbos is a taste of *Olam Haba.*

L'khah Dodi
Oh Friends, Good Friends

t is difficult to imagine that there was a time when the hymn composed by Shlomo HaLevi Alqabetz[16] was not part of the Friday night Kabbalat Shabbat service. But the fact is that it was composed in the 1500s and originated in the circle of kabbalists in the city of Safed. I translated this Shabbat hymn to be sung alongside the Hebrew or freestanding in English.

Oh friends, good friends, the bride let's face,
The Shabbos Queen, in Her find space.

Shamor and *Zakhor*, the word was one.
Spoken by God unique and One,
Yah is One, Yah's name is One.
And glorious, gracious are Yah's ways.

Let's go to meet the Shabbos rest,
And deeply drink this fountain blessed.
Primeval Source contains the rest,
Omega, Alpha – all our days.

Majestic city, proudly rear
Your head, come forth, no need to fear.
No need to shed another tear –
Just yield and flow in mercy's grace.

Hope! Rise up from the dust of the earth.
Your radiant clothes proclaim your worth.
Mashiaḥ brings our own rebirth –
Our souls can feel redemption's rays.

---

16   Born c.1500, Thessaloniki, died 1580, Safed. *Shamor* is to protect/observe the Sabbath and *Zakhor* is to remember the Sabbath. The terms are references to the two different commands concerning the Sabbath found in the Torah.

Haloes waken you to light.
Wake up your mind with inner sight.
Sing and let your soul take flight –
On heaven's glory set your gaze.

Let go of pride, let go of shame,
Just steadfast be: there is no blame.
The poor find comfort in your name
And build the Lord's eternal place.

Victory fills your heart today.
Prevailing over past dismay.
God's joy will make you glad and gay,
As when the groom sees his bride's face.

You can expand on every side.
The Lord's anointed is your guide.
To God's domain, so rich and wide.
In joy, experience God's good grace.

Turn to face the open door
She comes to stay forever more.
Our people ready as before
To be again her dwelling place.

El Mistater
The Hidden God

In 1939, I found myself in Antwerp after fleeing from Austria in the wake of Hitler's invasion. There I met people who opened me up to God and spirituality. They were studying Chabad philosophy under the late Rabbi Moshe Tchechoval, of blessed memory. It was during those late Shabbat afternoon hours when we sat and sang the melodies conducive to the feeling of cleaving to God that I first heard the hymn below. The words were written by Rabbi Avraham Maimin,[17] a disciple of the great kabbalist Rabbi Moshe Cordovero, who preceded Rabbi Isaac Luria in the city of Safed. It is a hymn in celebration of the divine attributes, and we sang it to the melody that originated in the court of Hussyatin (of the Rhizin dynasty).

Almighty, well hidden, beyond reason's edge
In soft realms beyond where conscious thought can be met
Most High, Primal Cause crowned with *Keter's* bright light
A crown we and angels give You *Hvyh!*

Before You gave Torah to us Jews at first
Imprinted She was in Your *Hokhmah* arcane.
From naught She did come and then She was hid.
Hokhmah's first fruit is awe of You *Hvyh!*

Rivers of faith flowing broadly at once,
Deep waters, yield freely to the insightful one.
Binah's gates, fifty, do open to him —
Such insightful faith comes from You *Hvyh!*

Heavens grace pour on those who seek You
Whose eyes are forever looking for You
Abraham's God, please be mindful of us

---

17   Avraham Maimin, Safed, d. 1570? whose name is spelled out in the first letter of each verse - ABRHM MYMYN and each verse focuses on another of the Holy Emanations (*sefirot*).

Who praise You for *Ḥesed*, O benign *Hvyh*!
Mighty and strong with *Gevurah's* firm power
Extracting light from nought's place of exchange
Isaac's fright to our judgment bring light,
    You are the hero eternal *Hvyh*!

Mysteriously great is Your Mercy's own work
Jacob's strength mixing kindness with awe.
    Tiferet of Israel You hear our prayer.
Who else hears the poor except You *Hvyh*!

Yah, may parent's merit protect us from harm.
    Netzaḥ of Israel redeem us from woe.
Raise us from the pit of the exile's abyss
That we too may work for Your plan *Hvvh*!

Meeting of right and of left in the words
Of prophets receiving from *Netzaḥ* and *Hod*
Yakhin and Boaz these pillars are named
    As all of Your children learn You *Hvyh*!

Yesod is the *Tzaddik* one hidden in seven
The sign of the pact with the world is She,
The fount of blessing is at the world's base.
    You are the *Tzaddik*, the Manroot *Hvvh*!

Now raise *Malkhut* up to David and his son
Crown him as Mother *Sh'khina* did and as She will.
    Israel is named bride and pleasant is She.
The crown and the splendor are in Your hand *Hvyh*!

Ḥazak You contain the ten *S'firot* in One.
If one be cut off no light will be seen.
When together they are then bright is their light
Accept me and my song too, my Lord *Hvyh*!

Libbi u-V'sari
My Heart and My Flesh[18]

Rabbi Avraham Ibn Ezra[19] wrote this hymn, whose refrain "my heart and my flesh they sing to you my God" engraved itself on my heart. I first heard it from my teacher-friends in Antwerp in 1939. I want other people to be able to share these deep feelings engendered by this poem, which was originally written to be a preface to the *Nishmat* (page 22).

All potent God! You made me
"Alive I am," You told me
yet no one's eyes can see Me
remaining flesh – alive
my heart and my flesh
they sing to You,
to You the Source of Life!

Brought forth we were by intent
in counsel and consent
yet hidden is what this meant
from us who are alive.

Resplendent in Your glory
all tales are but Your story
praise to You who is pouring
into our souls our life!
How generous on Your side
to teach us laws which guide
those who by them abide
as sources of good life!
Might we be ever right

---

18   The acrostic reads: ABRaHaM BeN EZRA
19   Rabbi Avraham ben Meir ibn Ezra was born at Tudela, Spain in 1089 and died c. 1164 apparently in Calahorra. He was one of the most distinguished Jewish men of letters and writers of the Middle Ages. He excelled in philosophy, astronomy/astrology, poetry, linguistics, and exegesis; he was called *The Wise, The Great* and *The Admirable Doctor*.

and live all in the light
what are we but a mite
and yet You give us life!

Born as we are of passion
at times we lack compassion
if only we could fashion
a God-filled way of life!

Near God to be we yearn
from wicked ways to turn
before bodies to dust return
and souls to the Source of Life

Every way will I adore You
my fervent prayer implore You
to open my path before You
to sate my soul with life!

Zeal filled our sires with fervor
do rouse us from our torpor
and help us meet our savior
of Jesse's stock – in Life!

Remember! we kept Your trust
may Your response be just
and being fair You must
decree us toward life!

Awed am I, amazed at You
my arms I raise in pray'r to You
my mouth will sing its praise to You
O Source and Soul of Life!

The Shabbat Table Hymns

Rabbi Yitzḥak Luria[20]

The twenty-six hours (twenty-six being the numeric value of YHVH) of Shabbat are divided into three distinct periods or moods or rhymes. Each one is represented by a different type of prayer service, a different type of meal, and a different type of melody. Rabbi Luria composed three Shabbat hymns that encapsulate the mystical dimensions of this triad.

1. Hymn for Friday Night[21]

In the Song of Songs (2:3), it says, "Underneath the apple tree I have aroused you." This becomes the reference for the period of Friday night, representing the conjugal union of the Holy One, blessed be He, and His consort, the *Shekhinah*. In this song, there are many allusions to that sacred union in the aspect of the Shabbat which is grounded in the *sefirah* of *Malkhut*. It represents the homecoming to the aspect of the Mother – the Queen, the Bride, the *Shekhinah* – and it is usually celebrated in the mood of loving and warm conviviality.

O sing – give praise!
Enter the gates
of the orchard paradisial and holy.

Now bid her to enter –
Life-loaf and light,
with aureoles garlanded, we're ready.

---

20   The sixteenth century Kabbalist, Rabbi Yitzḥak Ben Solomon Luria (1534-1572) revolutionized the study of Jewish mysticism through Kabbalah. Luria, also known as Isaac Ashkenazi, attracted a large number of followers who gave him the title of "HaAri," The Lion, because of the initials of the phrase "Haeloki Rabbi Yitzḥak" — the divine Rabbi Yitzḥak.

21   The acrostic reads: ONY YSHC LURIA BN ShLMH – I am Yitzḥak Luria the son of Shlomo

You fair bride surrounded
on right and on left
wrapped regally bejewelled and sharing.

Yon husband embraced one,
fundamentally held,
ecstatically blissfully crushed.

Surrendered are pains,
Silent the screams,
Joy aspects replacing the painful.

New radiance, new joy,
are given this day,
souls once more are added to spirits.

Heights of delight are scaled,
one-ing and two-ing;
light reaches Her fully and blessing.

Come close, entertain Her;
serve dainties and fish snacks,
deck festive the board of our banquet.

Let soul be the essence,
each spirit renewed,
two-ing and three-ing in clusters.

Upon her crowns seventy,
and holy, most holy,
the King is wrapped in splendor, high glory.

Resplendent, yet hidden
within all the worlds,
transcending all days yet indwelling.

I plead with Him
that He dwell with His folk,
honeymooning and joying sweetly.

At south's side my banquet,
by lights of arcane love,
the loaves crisp at north's side abundant.

Betrothed and her lover,
each feeding the other,
sustain each with fragrance of myrtle.

New garlands of love talk:
How precious the Kiddush
of seventy words over fifty.

Shekhinah surrounded,
six loaves on each side,
entangled, yet all recollected.

Shut off and forsaken,
the uglies are banished,
pains, hurts and wounds are no longer.

Let us then break bread
a morsel from each loaf.
Thus two Yuds the secret make clearer.

Mills grind the pure olives,
oil silently flows on,
in rivers interior and hidden.

Have secrets to share,
and words darkly hidden,
arcane, unseen by eyes mortal.

I crown you bride holy,
with secrets supernal,
at this mating feast of the angels.

2. Hymn for Shabbat Noon[22]

The Zohar teaches us that on Shabbat morning the effulgence of the Ancient of Days (*Attik Yomin*) is present. This second meal is consumed after the morning liturgy. In the *mussaf* liturgy, the sanctification (*kedushah*) we begin with the words, *keter yitnu lekha* pointing to the utter transcendent realm of *Keter*, the highest of the *sefirot*. Having read the Torah, we are in a more contemplative, more cerebral mood, and here Luria alludes to the high sharing of secrets.

On Sabbath's morn
This feast is set
God beyond All
Presides this time.

Now Souls rejoice
The cup is full
The hallowing vast
The halo bright.

Your glory is cast
Your precious sight
Secrets whispered
You share with us.

You give us the clue
To breads ten and two
Breathed out and in
Two letters of thy name.

Supernal bond
All life's warrant
Its pow'r increased
To the highest raised.

---

22   The acrostic reads: ONY YSHQ LURIA – I am Yitzḥak Luria

Husbands of Earth
Joy in full voice
And speak the word
As honey sweet.

Quotes new and bold
Before the Kind of old
Of lore arcane
Reveal the same.

Let's garland this table
With dear secret fable
Profoundly related
Not openly stated.

Up, up to the skies
These words help us rise
And there to find ease
The sun's healing rays.

Rich increase appears
Beyond ranks that are carved
Mates once separated
Now fully are mated.

In this rhyme of Luria's
Two stanzas are left
Incomplete by the author
On purpose I think.

All will be completed
When all is completed
Until we are redeemed
These remain deleted.

3. Hymn for Shabbat Afternoon[23]

On Shabbat afternoon, the six sefirot (*Ḥesed, Gevurah, Tiferet, Netzaḥ, Hod, Yesod*) are in ascendance. It is also a time for the manifestation of the pure Divine grace that casts no shadow. Those who participate in this third meal are often concerned with the impending week and sing this song of Luria's with great longing. Rabbi Menahem Mendel of Kotzk once said: "The Rabbis have said that one hour of *t'shuvah* (repentance) and good deeds in this world is greater than all the joys of the World-to-Come. Which hour is this hour? The hour of the third meal."

The Courtiers of God
Who long to see
The glory of the One Impatient.

You see engraved
On this table top
The seal of the King most Holy.

So decreed all are one
At this great conclave,
Surrounded by angelic hosts.

Have joy at these times;
His benevolence shines
All wrath is gone all is still.

Come nigh and see
The power is mine,
No harshness accuses you now.

Let snarling dogs leave!
Outcast them complete,
No longer admit them on high.

---

23   The Acrostic reads: YSHC LURYA – Yitzḥak Luria

Until *minḥa* time
He patiently waits
For change to be taking place.

Removing all shells –
His will them dispels –
His own, He reveals now in full.

Yes, holed up they stay,
Held down in dismay.
No quarter to them is now given.

Arrayed now is He
In joy impatiently
For the time when the week won't return.

Yom Zeh L'Yisra'el
Your Gift to Those Who Strive with You

Rabbi Yitzḥak Luria

It is amazing how much teaching of consciousness, sublime cosmology, and sacred psychology has come down to us through the channel of Rabbi Isaac Luria,[24] of blessed memory. The enormous body of his legacy comes to us through his disciples, chiefly Rabbi Ḥayim Vital Calabrese, who served as his amanuensis. Nevertheless, some of the sacred table hymns are likely to have been written by the Lion himself. This particular hymn is a devotional romance of praise to the Sabbath and is easily accessible to families around the Sabbath table.

This version works best when sung to a Flamenco tune and the English version is done simultaneously with the Hebrew.

י

Your gift
to those who strive with You
is joy and light
Shabbat Menuḥah.

צ

Certain of Your holy ways
You revealed to us at Sinai
Shabbat and other holy days
we are to keep as You commanded
You send your healing rays
accept our human ways
Shabbat Menuḥah.

---

24   His name Yitzḥak Luria in Strength is spelled out in Hebrew and English from the first letters of each verse.

ח

Charm is Shabbat for the heart
for the poor and broken people
if all week we were depressed
additional souls are ours on Shabbat
to help our anxious moods
breathe a relaxing sigh
Shabbat *Menuḥah.*

ק

Consecrated bride You blessed
all other days gave her their blessing
in the sixth and final phase
You finished global creation
There found the sorrowing
calm and security
Shabbat *Menuḥah.*

ל

Let go of every form of toil
You in Your kindness have commanded
regal auras shine from us
when we keep Shabbat as is wanted
I offer holy gifts
a fragrant sacrifice
Shabbat *Menuḥah.*

ו

What songs of love could I perform
with rhythm and harmony and music
to please your presence holy God?
My soul delights in her surrender
Do keep that promise God
to your beloved folk
Shabbat *Menuḥah.*

ר

Receive my worship blessed God
as if it was my life I offered
This restful, blissful Shabbat day
with ample joy and sweet elation
we feel secure and loved
in Your protection God
Shabbat *Menuḥah.*

י

Your salvation do we trust
Yah God most powerful and mighty
David's heirs – do send them soon
to those who must transcend convention
Let Freedom be proclaimed
and with it space that's safe
Shabbat *Menuḥah.*

א

Awesome God who is most High
do look for us and give an answer
Redeem this troubled planet soon
Be kind and manifest Your caring
Revive our trust in You
with light and blissfulness
Shabbat *Menuḥah.*

ת

Cherish and Renew Your house
enough the years it was in shambles
With Your compassion Gentle God
console the grieving ones in sorrow
who puts her grief aside
to sing You Shabbat songs
Shabbat *Menuḥah.*

ז

Zealous to treasure this holy day
keep us well in your remembrance
Protect and guard us wondrous God
this day and every other day
Beloved do respond
and grant deliverance
Shabbat *Menuḥah.*

ק

Could celebration's welcome song
be heard by Israel and her neighbors
when that vast vision is fulfilled
and all the world is safe from terror
Our light has dawned this day
and shines in every way
Shabbat *Menuḥah.*

Yom Shabbaton Eyn Lishko'aḥ
The Unforgettable Sabbath Day

In all likelihood, this beautiful song was composed by the great poet, Yehudah HaLevi.[25] The refrain about the dove of Noah is a delight to children, who love to sing it. There are many melodies that have been composed for this song. YeHUDaH is spelled out in the acrostic.

> **י** You, dear Shabbat, are always here for me;
> How fragrant you linger in my awareness.
> Noah's dove found rest and so can we,
> Weary ones from the toil of the week.

> **ה** Honored are you by us, the believers,
> Parents and children, who keep you with zeal.
> Powerful is its message on the Tablets of stone;
> We sing your praises in prayer and at meals.

> **ו** When at the Mount Sinai in covenant we pledged
> We promised in one voice to do and to listen,
> Responding to Your challenge we answered together:
> You God are the One who imbues us with strength.

> **ד** Dear and Holy at Sinai you spoke to us;
> "Remember and Keep this Day one of Seven,
> When fully you keep the Shabbat together,
> You will be refreshed and with vigor imbued.

> **ה** How just like a lost sheep, so aimless, you wandered
> Remember the Shabbat your promise and pledge
> No evil will hurt you if you keep the Shabbat
> My rainbow will hold you in safety forever."

25   Spanish philosopher and Hebrew poet; born in Toledo, southern Castile, in the last quarter of the eleventh century; died in the Land of Israel in 1140.

Yedid Nefesh
You who love my soul[26]

R abbi Eleazar Azikri[27] was also among the people of the Safed Circle. This devotional love song to God is one of the most sublime calls of longing for union with God, the lover. Among Ḥasidim, there have been a number of yearning melodies to fit to this poem. I have been graced to learn a melody claiming to come from the Ba'al Shem Tov. While people will be singing this hymn before the Kabbalat Shabbat service in Hebrew, I felt the need for the translation to be sung either by itself or simultaneously with the Hebrew, in order that the people who sing it could get to the feeling expressed by the author in their own hearts.

> ׳   You who love my soul
Compassion's gentle source,
Take my disposition and shape it to Your will.
Like a darting deer I will flee to You.
Before Your glorious Presence
Humbly do I bow.
Let Your sweet love
Delight me with its thrill
Because no other dainty
Will my hunger still.

> ה   How splendid is Your light
Which worlds do reflect!
My soul is worn from craving
For Your love's delight.
Please, good God, do heal her

---

26   The acrostic spells out the Holy name Y - H - W - H.
27   Eleazar Azikri was a Safed kabbalist (1533-1600). He was the author of *Sefer Ḥaredim* (The Book of the Godfearers), in which the precepts are given an original classification corresponding to the various organs and limbs of the body with which they are carried out.

And show to her Your face,
So my soul can see You
And bathe in Your grace.
There she will find strength
And healing in this sight.
Her joy will be complete then
Eternal her delight.

ו   What pity stirs in You
Since days of old, my God!
Be kind to me Your own child
Begotten by Your love.
For long and longing hours
I yearned for Your embrace
To see my light in Your light
Basking in Your grace.
My heart's desire is
To harmonize with Yours
Do not conceal Your pity
Hide not that light of Yours.

ה   Help, my Lover, spread
Your canopy of peace.
Enfold all human beings
Give all pain surcease.
Your presence on this earth plane
Do make known to us
And we shall respond then
With song and with dance.
Rush, my love, be quick,
The time for love is now,
Let Your gentle favor
Grace us as of old...

Eshet Ḥayil
For An Accomplished Woman

(Proverbs 31:10-31)
To my beloved Ḥavah Raḥel

It is the custom on Friday night to serenade the woman of the house after greeting the angels and before the Kiddush. Although King Solomon had difficulty finding one woman among thousands to praise, he had no difficulty praising his mother with the poem below. According to the mystical tradition, at times King Solomon is the stand-in for God, the King of Peace, and the accomplished woman, the *Shekhinah*, with whom God is greatly pleased. By chanting this song, one praises both the mistress of the home as well as the *Shekhinah*.

א An accomplished woman who can find;
beyond pearls is your worth.
ב By your integrity your husband's heart is secure;
nothing is lacking where you are in charge.
ג Good are you to me, never vexing,
all your days (and especially our nights).
ד Designing in wool and linen,
your hands do your bidding with alacrity.
ה High business acumen is yours,
like that of a world trader,
importing food from afar.
ו Well before dawn you rise
to apportion meals for our family
and tasks for your helpers.
ז Zealously you assess your purchases before buying;
a vineyard you plant, the fruit of your hands
ח How mightily you gird your loins.
Your embraces are warm and strong.
ט Tastily, you offer your wares;

your light radiates undimmed through the night.
י Your hands are firm in what they weave together;
your palms support the spinning wheels.
כ Kindly, you support the poor,
your hands at the service of the needy.
ל Lily white clean is our home
and brightly colored its appointments.
מ Many textured are your weaves;
you wear silks and purples in elegance.
נ Named and known am I as your husband
when I sit in the councils of the elders.
ס Sheer are the garments you design;
your enterprise is valued by the people.
ע On you dresses become beauty and strength,
and your future is happily assured.
פ Pearls of wisdom come from your lips;
your speech is gentle and kind.
צ Certain is the way you conduct our home,
and immaculate is our kitchen.
ק Courteous are your relatives and friends in their praise of you,
and your husband raves about you.
ר Ravishing and skillful are many good women,
but you are even more stunning than they.
ש Shameless is mere charm and mere dazzling is vain.
How you are in God awareness, that is worth extolling!
ת Thousand-fold may you reap your rewards
for your fame deserves to be widely acknowledged.

Tzur Mishelo
From You, the Everlasting...

This table hymn, whose author is not known to me, is based on the four parts of the *Birkat Hamazon*—the Grace after Meals. The rule is that giving thanks for the food that we have eaten is a scriptural commandment; moreover, this obligation can be fulfilled in any way and in any language in which it is expressed. So, some people sing this song in place of the *Birkat Hamazon*.

Hashem you fed us dinner
Let us all give thanks
We ate and we are sated
The gift of your hands.

You nurture us and others
Our shepherd and our host
We ate of Your bounty
And drank of your vineyards
Now we give our thank-yous
With the mouth
That ate Your food
Singing and praising
Your holy repute.

We sing to You our God
We offer You our thanks
For earth and her harvest
With which we are gifted
Our souls are also glad
For the plenty that we had
Your love fills our being
Your truth fills our mind.

We need Your kind attention
So needy are Your folk
To come to Your Temple
On Zion's holy Hill
May David's heir redeem us
May he soon arrive
We long for his redeeming
To reinvigorate our life.

Your holy house rebuild now
Let Zion's streets be filled
New music will we make
New songs we all will sing
Compassionate of Blessings
We sing to you our grace
And raise our cup of thankfulness
For Your presence in our lives.

Yah Ekhsof Noam Shabbat
Longing for the Bliss of Shabbat [28]

A Shabbat Hymn by Reb Aaron the Great of Karlin

Rabbi Aaron of Karlin the Great,[29] one of the foremost disciples of the Maggid of Mezeritch, wrote this beautiful hymn. With the words he composed a melody, which has the power to stir the heart and raise up the soul. It has been adopted by many Ḥasidim and is sung at the third meal of the Shabbat. The acrostic spells out the holy name of God.

> **Y**ah! How I long for the bliss of the Shabbat,
> United in secret with Your own fervent wish.
> Give way to Your own deep desire to love us.
> May Shabbat in Torah be our sacred bliss.
> Share Her with us who desire to please You —
> Our deep thirst for union be met with delight.

> **H**oly Presence that fills time and space!
> Keep safe who keep Shabbat in their longing all week.
> Like a deer that seeks water by the banks of the river,
> We seek Shabbat, the secret of Your sacred Name!
> Grant us all week long Her shimmering Presence,
> So our hearts and our faith be pure service to You!

> **W**armly embrace us with Your kind compassion,
> Quench quickly our thirst for Your unending Grace.
> Give us the bliss drink from Eden's own river.
> Your praises we sing with joy on our face.
> Let Jacob's gift to us – echo all week long
> Infusing our lives with a Shabbat-filled trace.

---

28   The acrostic spells out the Holy name Y – H – W – H.
29   Rebbe Aaron HaGadol (The Great) of Karlin (1736—1772)

Hail Shabbat, delight of our souls and our Spirits.
Ecstasy life-throb I am awed by Your love,
Secure In Your caring there is safety and nurture –
You feed us sweet nectar from Your Source above.
As You embrace us with Mothering comfort –
In You I take refuge and pledge You my love.

III

Prayers from the Days of Awe

Tishrey
The Year is Nearly Gone

The approach of the High Holy Days asserts into the heart and mind a sense of ominous poignancy. In quiet moments, in which one reviews the past year, the soul looks into the mirror to assess itself before entering into the time when God makes Divinity present to us. This examination of conscience – Ḥeshbon Hanefesh – led me to muse in the words below.

The year is nearly gone.
What was it all about?
My God what did it mean?
We wrestled You and I.
Did it have a purpose, what we did?

At this hour of prayer
Time for looking in
I seek You to show me
Once again the vision You
Showed me in those days.

And yet in this abandonment
In which I seek You and only
Me I find in the seeking
And I know that underneath
The seeker's knowing there are You!

So show Your face and hide it not
I beg You. And You in me beg me to
Show You the move, the very next
Which I would have You guide me to
The one surprise You crave.

That I, not in aforethought schemes,
Though goody-good, please You, taking
Instead loving risk, to leap in faith,
In hope, despite the deep despair,
From the learning I gathered from my bruise'd life.

Still juggling I am forced to dance
My frantic dance to balance tasks
You laid on me in kids and kisses
And often something falls, I miss
To catch an obligation I took on.

Then I fail, and hear You laughing at me.
I rage at this, so full of failure,
Once again I slipped. I did not manage
To do it right – If only then I could give ear
To the sigh You sigh in me,
And see that the laugh is kind,
Not gloating at my failure.
A forgiving chuckle in which You
Thank me for the pratfall that
Showed I tried my best.

And all too short my reach was then,
I missed – You laughed, a *Purim shpiel*
Purim/Kippurim – somehow alike?
Mordeḥai/Haman – start again
And juggle on. You Zalman laugh also!

You urge me to see the joke, it was on me,
My turn to enter-tain not main-tain.
Not taint you dummy! Stop the guilt.
The milk that spilled was not in vain,
God's gain that laugh, forever will remain.

In solitude, eternally confined,
I need you woman, man and child
That I may pour my self into

You to wrestle/love my me as me,
My me as you. And in the laugh,

It's done I'm one. I doubly cloned.
Am now at-one-ed when sinner, sin
And sinning one. There is no victim.
Gone is the shame you felt.
The Uni-/-verse is my playroom and yours.

Will you come and be with me in me,
In the Sukkah of wholeness? Let us again
Fall in love and dance and visit with
The fathers three, the mothers four and dance
The dance *Breisheet - Kol Yisrael* once more.

Seliḥah
Sorrow, How I missed You!

Isaac b"r Judah Ibn Gayyat (1038–1089)

I was so amazed when I first recited this *Seliḥah*.[30] I had often found a comparable kind of Eros in the Baul songs of India, the Qawwali music of the Sufis, and the spousal mysticism of Teresa of Avila and Mechthild of Magdeburg. So it should not have been such a surprise; after all, the Song of Songs, which is the inspiration for this poem of Ibn Gayyat, is even more explicit in its romantic Eros, and didn't Rabbi Akiba point out that although many sacred songs are holy, the Song of Songs is the Holy of Holies? Therefore, I felt urged to translate it for those who cannot read it in the original Hebrew. (All translation is necessarily an interpretation – so let me share mine with you.)

> I must return to my very first lover
> Like an eye's pupil He kept me safe
> Tall is my beloved like a cedar
> I can't sleep when I think of Him.
>
> How he rescued me from vile hands
> How He wed me in all new robes
> Speaking to me in holy words
> Honoring me with Sacred pact.
>
> Endowering me with ample boon
> Amidst many joys, delights supreme
> Our tryst He stocked for intimacy
> Countless lasses in waiting He set to serve me
> The choicest foods to fulfill His pledge.

---

30   Penitentiary prayer expressing sorrow and asking for forgiveness said during the period of the New Year.

In His inner chambers He cleaved to me
While in the courtyards they spiced the air
My Royal Lover took me into His chambers.
And I, bathed to purity my scent arousing
He mounted our couch and between my breasts
He laid, embraced me and held me...

And in the wink of an eye it happened
All broken – betrayed – as I went off
With attitude defiant, mocking, and dazed.

My Lover, now disengaged, was gone.
My guts wrenched, keening for my Dear One
What was it that I upset? What drove Him away?
He is gone now and no comfort left me.

How I sought Him to no avail,
Called Him to no response,
Do turn back My Lord, I wailed,
He had gone and I waited in vain hope.
While my heart cried like a sad violin.

My eyes in tears that do not dry
I lost my dignity, I felt degraded
Besmirched and defiled, foul and dirty
Thrown, tossed about and despised.

Like a young widow I hoped
For the day of comfort
My vulnerable need has turned to frustration
Flames of longing have become a wall
O Mercy, Please, for one not pitied.

Come back, come back O Shulamit
Freed from your hurt, from Your desolation
I your Maker seek to behold you, come quick
Lift your feet and swiftly come from Lebanon
We are reconciled, arouse your love again

I your Lover will restore you,
You shall know clearly the face of Your flock
Zion, the glorious, do grant her
The goodness of Your desire
Your devotees will sing
And acclaim the adventure –
Yes, You heard my voice!
You did not avert Your Ear.

Abba, Abba Have Pity!

The literal translation of *tekiah* is 'blast!'; the literal translation of *shevarim* is 'break!'; and the literal translation of *teruah* is 'shatter!' All the commentators tell us that the sound of the shofar[31] – the ram's horn – should be *kol pashut* – 'a simple note.' In my imagination, I see a tone generator that begins with a note that gets interrupted on an ever more frequent interval to the point where the interruptions are no longer noticeable and we are right back with what sounds like the original, continuous note.

In the '60s and '70s, some psychologists were advocating primal scream therapy. When I heard the teaching of the Ba'al Shem that the sound of the shofar means 'Abba, Abba have pity' – the call of the soul to the father – I wrote the piece below and read it with my congregation as an introduction to the sounding of the shofar on Rosh Hashanah.

Said the Ba'al Shem Tov
Tekiah –
a simple scream
Abba, Abba have pity!
Abba, Abba save!
And this simple scream
needs no words,
no further modulation,
only to scream
so as to unite
with the sound of Creation
and the thunder of Revelation
and the calling of Redemption
The great AMEN.

31   The sounds of the shofar consist of: *Tekiah* – one note; *Shevarim* – three short notes; and *Teruah* – nine staccato notes. These are strung together in the following pattern: *Tekiah Shevarim Teruah Tekiah* repeated three times. Then *Tekiah Shevarim Tekiah* repeated three times. Then *Tekiah Teruah Tekiah* repeated three times with the final note being extended to become: The Great Blast!

Tekiah is the name
and the grace of Abraham.
He is kind and warm and gentle.

Shevarim is the name *Elohim*,
and the terror of Isaac,
his sighs
at the binding on the altar.
He is afraid yet wants to take our place
in the rigors of the judgment.

And *Teruah* is Jacob,
all broken into tribes,
his weeping for Rachel, for Joseph,
for Dinah, for Shimon;
His blessing for which he had to
risk so much
yet also the Compassion of Y-H-V-H.

Grace—Rigors—Mercy—Grace
Grace—Rigors—Grace
Grace—Mercy—Boundless Grace

All begins and ends in grace
Thus in the deepest, least verbal way
the ear can hear
the heart can be at one
the innards are stirred
and together they scream.
Abba, Abba take pity!
Abba, Abba save!

So we scream as loud as we can
and echo the shofar
in a way no one but G-d can hear
Abba, Abba pity, save!

Kol Nidre
All Our Promises

While the *Kol Nidre* is basically a legal formula, over the years it has taken on much more of an aura of solemnity. The melody is haunting, but because it is often performed as a concert-like piece, people are not aware of its transformative intent. In Hasidic sources, the notion of making a vow does not receive much positive reinforcement. It is seen as a last resort of a moral weakness. The problem is that when we make vows and do not keep them, we not only transgress a Divine command, but also whatever word we give becomes hollow and often meaningless. Knowing this, we want to create a safety net at this solemn moment and declare it once we have found out about making vows.

Before we begin
to atone for last year
we make clear
that we know
how we vow.
Our word to keep
we mean indeed
which we give
when we want
to bribe God
with good deeds.

So we state
that next year
we will with less fear
live our weakness and strength
as it flows.
No more vows,
no more bribes.
no more oaths
will we pledge.

And if in weakness we vow
we do void them right now
so that freely
we serve God and Man.

By consent
of this group
gathered here
in this space
and consent
of the powers
on high,
we will share
in this prayer
and admit
we were wrong
all together
and apart
you and I.

A light which transcends
all limits and bounds
is sown in our hearts
at this time.
Thus the *Tzaddik* in us
can rejoice and be glad
and burst forth
from our eyes
now and shine!

T'shuvah
Coming Back Around

Many years ago—from 1952 to 1956—I served an Orthodox congregation in New England. The makeup of the people who came to the services was seven percent older immigrants from a small town in Lithuania, while the rest were people who joined because it was less expensive than the Conservative congregation. Their Jewish quotient of knowledge was very low. Many of them worked as engineers and middle managers in the factories of the town. I felt that I needed to have a way of singing something with them before I would begin my homily on the Days of Awe. I also wanted to have a melody they would easily be able to join in with. In those days, many people still remembered a Yiddish song, "*A Brivele der Mammen*"—about a letter to a mother in Europe from her son in America. These lyrics could be sung with a feeling of longing and nostalgia for a better life. That was just the right thing to open hearts before offering my message.

A year has gone by,
I say with a sigh –
O Lord I did not progress.
Your Torah not learned,
Your *Mitzvot* not earned,
This I am forced to confess.

I undertake
This to remake
My life anew to fashion.
So help me, please,
From sin to cease
And only to You
Give my passion.

I seek Your light,
I need Your aid.
Without Your joy
I am afraid.
Heal me God
In body and in soul.

Please, good God,
Pour out Your blessing,
That in Your sight
We'll be progressing.
O Lord above,
Let us feel Your love
And perceive You,
Our souls caressing.

May we not be
Disappointed
In waiting for ben David
Anointed.
With Your open hand,
Bless our Holy Land
And our leaders
Whom we have appointed.

Yah Melekh
God is King, God was King, God will always be King

Some of the religious poems that make up the High Holy Day liturgy come in the form of a litany with some phrases repeated. It is unknown who took from various Bible verses and created this mantric formula that stretches the Divine realm into times from before the Big Bang to after the last black hole of the universe. The Divine present is from the Big Bang to the last black hole. What happened before is the Divine past. What will happen after the last black hole is the Divine future. And so, in the contemplation of eternity, the poet put together an alphabetical litany that pointed to the angelic servants of God and how they might celebrate God's sovereign rule. Using a snappy folk tune, I offered the rendition below. Whenever we do this in the synagogue, it brings smiles and childlike delight to those who sing along.

Awesome Angels	Answer in a call	Yah *Melekh*
Beautiful Beings	Boast in their call	Yah *Malakh*
Cheerful Cherubim	Chant in their call	Yah *Yimlokh L'olam Va'ed*

Dominant	Delegates	Deliver a call
Eminent	Effulgences	Exclaim and call
Fabulous	Familiars	Flare and call

Gregarious	Gleamers	Glow and call
Holy	Heavenly hosts	Hallow and call
Ideal	Immanents	Issue a call

Jovial	Jubilators	Join in song and call
Keepers of	Karma	Corroborate and call

Loving	Luminaries	Light forth and call
Magnificent	Mediators	Modulate their call
Numinous	Naturals	Nurture us and call
Operatic	Organizers	Offer praise and call
Qabbalistic	Queen's attendants	Quote praise and call
Radiant	Rescuers	Rejoice and call
Sublime	Seraphim	Serenely sound their call
Triumphant	Tribute givers	Trumpet and call
Ubiquitous	Umpires	Ululate and call
Vibrant	Venerators	Voice their call
Well-meaning	Worshippers	Warble and call
Xstatic	xcellences	Exclaim and call
Yah adoring	Zodiac Ḥayot	Zestfully call.

El Melekh Yoshev
The Thirteen Attributes Of Mercy

The High Holy Day prayer book used by Conservative synagogues since the 1930s have incorporated many renditions and translations of prayers shaped in Victorian England. The language was stately and dignified with its 'vouchsafes' and 'bestows'. In the penitential sections of the *Seliḥot* prayers recited prior to *Rosh Hashanah*, and then much of the prayers on *Yom Kippur*, we recall the formula that as we read it in the Bible that God gave to Moses to bring about forgiveness for the sin of the Golden Calf. These thirteen Attributes of Mercy have been given the power to open the gates for our prayers, even if they are closed due to our sins. For this reason, the Hebrew formula in the liturgy is frequently repeated. I found this translation in the Conservative High Holy Day prayer book, adjusted it so that it could be more accessible to us in our day, and placed the acrostic to the Divine name in it. I composed a simple hymn-like melody so that we could sing this at least once during the series of repetitions, so that people would have an inkling of the content.

י

You sit firm in Your judgment seat
Enthroned on high,
And one by one our trespasses
In *t'shuvah* pass You by.
Almighty King, Your governing
Is with tender love replete.
Absolve we pray, our fears allay,
With mercy judgment mete.

ה

How high You dwell, our Rock and Shield,
Enthroned in might,

And you forgive each one their sins,
From scarlet You make white.
O Ruler wise, before Your eyes,
Our frailties stand revealed.
Your judgment be with empathy,
Your might with mercy wield.

ו

When first You taught Your attributes
Thirteen for us to say.
Remember then Your covenant
With us unto this day.
O living Fount, on Sinai's mount
You set Your nation's roots.
The truth, Your seal, You did reveal,
And none Your word refutes.

ה

How You did hold in holy glow
Your prophet Moses there.
Invoked he then Your name, O God,
And thus did You declare;
Yud Heh Vav Heh, Yud Heh Vav Heh
To wrath and anger slow,
Forgiving sin, our hearts to win,
To thousands mercy show.

Ki Hineh Kaḥomer
We Are As Clay In Potter's Hand

Here we have a beautiful hymn comparing our contingency at the hands of God. Based on a biblical phrase (Jer. 18:6), an unknown poet took this simile and expanded it to show the various forms of how we are the handiwork of the Creator. Often the word used to speak of God as Creator is *yotzer* – the same word is used for someone who shapes clay. I did not want people to be unaware of the content of the hymn. This one I also set to a simple musical form that is intended to bring out the meaning of the hymn.

We are as clay in potter's hand
He does contract, He does expand
So we are Yours to shape at will
We yield to You –
our passions still.

Like a mason shaping rough-hewn stone
We are Your stuff in flesh and bone
You deal with us in death, in life
We yield to You –
please heal our strife.

The smith can shape a blade of steel
Shape the edge and bend the heel
So through life's furnace you temper us
We yield to You –
surrender us.

A boat is steered by helmsman's might
He turns to left, he turns to right
As long as You keep straight our keel

We yield to You –
please make us feel.
As glass is shaped by blower's pipe
And vessels made of every type
So you shape us so we may contain
We yield to You –
in us remain.

As tapestry is formed thread by thread
And color is to texture wed
Our life is woven on Your loom
We yield to You –
save us from doom.

As jewelry is wrought from gold
And silver too is poured in mold
So You our souls have crafted, built
We yield to you –
erase our guilt.

Hosha'not
Save Us!

*H*osha'not are recited while walking with the *lulav*[32] and *etrog* around the Torah desk, each one on its day, each of the seven days of Sukkot. All seven are then recited again on *Hosha'na Rabba*—the Great *Hosha'na* Day— and in some communities these seven are also accompanied by the sounding of the shofar. This version, following the traditional one, is based on the seven days of the Creation story and follows the English ABC, while the traditional version has all the letters of the Alphabet and is based on other levels of interpretation of the quality of the days. The traditional version's *Hosha'not* of days 4, 5 and 6 have strong ecological concerns and were the encouragement to offer these.

For the first day – turn!

Hosha'na for the sake of
the Aura of life
the Beams of Light
the Clearness of Light
the Dynamics of Light
the Effulgence of Light
the Fractals of Light
the Glory of Light
the Haloes of Light
the Illumination of Light
the Joys of Sight.

---

32   The *lulav* and *etrog* refer to the four species that are collectively carried and waved together during the autumn festival of *Succot* — Tabernacles. The *lulav* is a palm frond from the very center of the palm tree, the *etrog* is a citrus fruit, the *aravot* are two branches from the willow tree, and the *hadasim* are three branches from the myrtle bush.

For the second day – turn!

Hosha'na for the sake of
the Karma of the separation of sky and water
the Luminosity of the sky
the Majesty of the sky
the Nourishment that comes in rain from the sky
the Orient and Occident in the sky
the Purple sunset sky
the Quality of purity of the sky
the Range of the sky
the Stretch of the firmament of the sky
the Treasures of rain that pour from the sky.

For the third day – turn!

Hosha'na for the sake of
the Ubiquity of the plants
the Variety of the plants
the Wellness of the plants
the Xanthia gum trees
the Yucca plants
the Zucchinis and Zinnias
the Aspen trees
the Berry bushes
the Chlorophyll made by the leaves
the Date palms.

For the fourth (Wednesday?) day – turn!

Hosha'na for the sake of
the Earth and planets
the Faraway stars
the Galaxies in space
the Horizons of the sky

the Infinity of space
the Joyous music of the spheres
the Komets and Asteroids
the Location of Latitude and Longitude on the maps
the Moons around the planets
the Nodes of the Zodiac.

For the fifth (Thursday?) day – turn!

Hosha'na for the sake of
Owls and Other Oviparous life
Perchs and Plovers
Quail and Quahaugs
Robins and Red Snappers
Seagulls and Swordfish
Turtles and Turtledoves
Univalves
Varieties of Plankton
Waterfowl and Whales
Yellowtails and Tunas.

For the sixth (Friday?) day – turn!

Hosha'na for the sake of
Zebus and Zebras
Aardvarks and Armadillos
Bears and Babies
Children and Chimpanzees
Deer
Elk and Moose
Fawns and Families
Giraffes and Gorillas
Homo Sapiens and Hominids
Instinctual and Intelligent life.

For the seventh (Shabbat?) day – turn!

Hosha'na for the sake of our
Letting Earth Rest
Letting Earth heal
Letting Earth recover
Leaving Earth in Peace
Letting People find their center
Letting People enjoy rest and freedom
Letting Children romp
Living the Shabbat in Mindfulness
Loving Others and Ourselves
Letting Being do all the Doing.

Maoz Tzur
My Salvation's Stronghold

he German melody we use for *Maoz Tzur*, traditionally sung after lighting the candles on each of the eight days of Ḥanukah, was taken from a Lutheran hymn. The usual translation that begins with the words "Rock Of Ages" also leaned on the Christian hymn that begins with the same words. The author Mordecai (as you can see from the acrostic of my translation) wrote this hymn not only for Ḥanukah but, as you can see, included the other Holy Days of the year. He followed the historic progression from Egypt to Ḥanukah. The final verse expresses the hope for the future redemption. Here I offer my translation which can still be sung to the meter of the Hebrew original.

מ My salvation's stronghold, fort
praising You is such delight.
Build your house of prayer, Lord,
cleansed from idols after fight.
You came to our assistance
when we gave resistance,
then we sang
a hymn of thanks
for your aid's persistence.

ר Ramparts, pyramids and forts
Egypt had us build for them.
We found no justice in their courts
when they drowned our children.
With grace beyond all measure
You redeemed Your treasure.
You split the sea
to help us flee
now Pesach is our pleasure.

ד Dear to us Your Temple was
still we could not tarry there.
Babylon's superior mass
exiled us we knew not where.
We drank that poisonous potion,
were moved in that commotion.
When we turned
we were not spurned
but gave You our devotion.

כ Keen was Haman's hate for us
when he was in power.
He vowed slaughter, death to us,
expecting us to cower.
To pride he kept clinging
while on the gallows swinging.
On that tree
meant for me.

י Ionian, Hellenist and Greek
did defile our holy place.
God did aid the faithful meek
who gave the enemy the chase.
Then they found new meaning
when they found in cleaning,
in their toil
some pure oil
Ḥanukah's beginning.

Holy aid extend to us,
and bring the end of exile soon.
When the foes oppressed the just
You protected us from doom
In an exile dour
at our darkest hour
Edom vain
lost its reign.
Make our Shepherd flower.

IV

Intercession

May you be a good intercessor for us.

This phrase is used in several leave-taking ceremonies. For instance, when a person would feel his or her end approaching, and the family would ask the person about to die to act as their emissary and plead for their needs before God. This phrase was also used before earth was placed over the coffin; and again when the mourners would rise from their *shiv'ah* (mourning) benches, walk out of the house through the front door and go to the farthest corner of their lot where they would say: "Your name was _____ on earth, do not forget us. Serve as an intercessor for us, and go on in peace."

Many of us would like to be able to serve our families after our passing. For one who believes in the reality of an afterlife, the responsibility of serving as an intercessor would be a pleasant one. But why wait? Wouldn't it be better to learn how to intercede for loved ones while still in the body?

In Jewish homes, the lighting of the Shabbat candles by the women is an occasion for such intercession. When I recall my sainted mother, I remember her tarrying at the Shabbat candles for close to an hour before she was through. I say it now with a smile, but really I felt it at that time, that she was instructing the good Lord in great detail what he might do for her children, grandchildren, and great grandchildren, as well as for other people on her prayer list. I had the sense that while my father was doing all the official 'you ought to' praying, my mother's prayers were the ones that were really effective on our behalf.

What would be a good way to do this intercession? For people who have experienced contemplation and meditation, active verbal prayer may seem the lesser mode; but it is a practice that has been used for millennia: often done quietly, the lips moving, the heart open, and the eyes overflowing with tears.

A Biblical example of this is Ḥannah, the mother of prophet Samuel, as she stood in the sanctuary with her lips moving and pouring out her heart in great devotion. From her we learn that there are three phases to intercession:

Phase One: *Placing oneself in the presence of God, whom we address with words of adoration and appreciation, affirming our belief in the miraculous order in which God can make changes for the better.*

Phase Two: *Holding up, in so many words, the results expected for the person for whom we are praying. It is important not to dwell too long on the difficult condition; one mentions it, but moves on as soon as possible to the desired results of healing and prosperity. At that point, it is good to mention things of merit, enumerating the good points of the person for whom one is praying. It is also important to put oneself in the condition that the colloquial 'put up or shut up' refers to; thus, offering charity or a meritorious act on behalf of the person for whom one is praying. This is the 'enter' button to submit that request.*

Phase Three: *Once, the great master, Reb Avraham Yehoshua Heschel of Apt was invited to attend a prayer meeting for rain and refused to go, saying, "I was watching all the people on the way to the synagogue, and not one of them brought an umbrella." That is to say, it is important to close the prayer of intercession with an affirmation in which one anticipates the good result; this is done with the tradition seal of 'Amen.'*

People who are not so sure about the existence of God, or who feel awkward in situations of verbal prayer, can reflect on the healing energies that our mother the earth sends to her children, provided they are not being interfered with by modes of living that are contrary to the natural flow. The mediator or intercessor can see him or herself as an accumulator, drawing down the healing energies that bring about relief and prosperity and directing them to the targeted person.

It is worth reading what Dr. Larry Dossey[33] and others who have written about the power of prayer, which is independent of time and distance, and has been empirically proven as useful. Even Buddhists who do not see themselves as theists, pray and intercede for the people in their lives through meditations like *tonglen*.

When a person practices intercession for a while, it becomes second nature. There are some prayers that don't need to take a lot of time in the tradition of intercessors; some of these prayers are called "arrow prayers." It has become my habit to offer such prayers whenever I hear sirens (in the affirmation that the rescue team will arrive in time to do good). Reading a headline in the newspaper or watching the news on the television, I do the same. I can't prove that my prayers will in actuality bring about great changes, but I sincerely believe that there would be a cumulative effect if many of us would do so at the same time.

I can't imagine that when my time comes that I would be unconcerned for the welfare of the people I left behind and would not assemble other spirits to join me as prayer partners for those whom I love.

The best way to intercede for others is when the words come directly from the heart to God. However, there are times when I feel that my own words fail me. So many requests for prayer have come to me that it is difficult to concentrate, to open my heart in compassion and to stay in touch with the details I want to bring into intercession. At such times, this prayer that I found in an old siddur, has helped me greatly. When I come to a particular phrase in the prayer, my memory opens to the concerns I have for the people on my prayer list. I suggest you become acquainted with this prayer. Use it and you will be glad that is available to you.

---

33   http://www.dosseydossey.com/larry/book.html

A Prayer For All Occasions

Our God, our parents' God
You hear the prayers
of our pleading
of all of us who turn to You.
May it please You
to hear also my own prayer.
I approach You and plead with You
knowing well
that I come without merit and worth
and without worthwhile deeds
I am embarrassed to raise my face to You,
to pray for myself and for other people –
yet it is Your boundless
compassion and kindness
that encourages me to trust
that You will not scorn me
but that You will support me
and come to my aid.

May my poor song
be pleasing to You
in hearing our prayers with compassion.
I come with a sore heart
to plead with You.
Please, in Your great compassion
take pity on the remnant
of Your people Israel
help us all and extricate us
from our confinements;
save us from our oppression;
help us to leave poverty and humiliation behind,
and keep us from a scarcity mentality;
protect us from all kinds of ruinous happenings
erupting upon the world.

Those who are healthy among us,
Your people Israel
guard them that no illness befall them,
no suffering enter them *Halilah!*

Those, among Your people,
the house of Israel who are ill,
hasten and send them a complete recovery.

Release all hostages to freedom
and save our people, the house of Israel,
from all pain and damage, assaults and accidents.
Compassionate One save us from such calamities.
Childless couples,
bless them with vigorous children,
proper, good and kosher offspring,
that are well thought of by You
and all the children of Your people.
May their parents,
their fathers and their mothers,
merit to raise them
to study Torah and to serve You, God,
so that they might walk in a straight path
and be attuned to awe of You.
Let no childhood disease take hold of them.
May they be protected
from demonic influences,
and from ill winds in the world,
from plagues and accidents,
so that they might be healthy and wholesome,
involved in serving You
and studying Torah all their lives.
Those mothers to be
who are carrying new life,
make them carry to term

in peace and without pain.
When the time for their birthing comes,
protect them from all hurt and damage;
help them through labor with ease
and without any complications.

Above all, may Your great mercy protect
the Exiled people Israel,
and the remnant of Your holy Torah.
May all who oppress them
become aware of Your retribution
and not shed innocent blood.

And may those of Your people Israel
who have gone astray
find ways to approach You again.
Receive them in complete *t'shuvah*.
Your right hand of grace
is stretched forth
to welcome those who repent.
Send us Your light and Your truth;
to guide us to live up to Your intention
in great compassion
help us to come home
and redeem us with a lasting redemption.
Amen *Selah!*

Prayer Before the Study of Kabbalah
Based on the Hebrew text of a disciple of Isaac Luria

My Lord, Creator of all,
Master of all worlds,
Supreme, compassionate and forgiving,
Thank You for Your Torah,
Thank You for allowing me to learn from it
And to move toward serving You.
Thank You for revealing some of the
Mysteries of Your Way.
I'm amazed this is truly happening to me.

Please forgive my foolishness and unkindness,
The sins of my past.
Sincerely I pledge to live more uprightly
That I may be ever closer to You.
Fill me with that awe of You that opens my capacity
For loving.
And open my heart to the mysteries
Of Your Holy Way.
Reveal Your Torah, I pray.

I pray too that this study will bring You joy.
It is the incense I offer in Your Holy Temple.
Bathe this my soul, Your Soul, in the light
Of the source of all.

Lord, please remember with me now, the kindness
And honesty of my ancestors who served You before.
Remember Your promise to care for the children
Of the righteous to the thousandth generation.
Enlighten me, if not for my own worth,
Then for theirs,
And for the future growth of Your people.

Let Your radiance be recognized today, now,
In me and through me, that I may use
The insights and energy of these,
Your Holy Teachings,
For the good of all living creatures
Everywhere, and for the furtherance
Of Your plan of the continuing creation.
Let no one anywhere be hurt by this study.
Guard my soul that it stays
On the straight path back to Your Home.

With King David, the joyful singer of Israel,
I pray "Open my eyes and let me see the
Wonders of Your Torah."
May the words of my mouth
And the meditation
Of my heart find favor before You, O Lord,
My Rock and my Redeemer.

Prayer for Yom Kippur *Katan*

The practice of prayer and penitence on Yom Kippur comes only once during the year. However, people who are serious about their spiritual life sought to experience Yom Kippur more often and dedicated the day before every new moon as a minor (*katan*) Yom Kippur.

You my God, my Helper
Ordering my life is not easy
My struggles are before You.

Keep at my side as I strive
I am not as good as I wish to be
Put forth Your light and lead me
Please guide my steps on Your path
Up to the level I can live on
Raise my actions to my values.

Kindness plant in my heart
Attention to the ways I am relating
To others who cross my path
And help me to live in balance
Neither in haste nor in sloth.

And give me joy in Your service
Making bright the lives
Of my loved ones
Embracing the lot You give me
Morning, noon and night
In Your service.

How may I come to You
If I did not heed Your word?

What You have made pure
I have polluted.
What You have loved
I despised.

What You have ordered
I have disrupted.
What you have intended
I have opposed.
Take my ways and turn them
So that I might make pure.

What I have polluted
That I may love What You love
That I may set to order What I have disrupted
That I might intend What You intend
May I be renewed
Like the moon.

May I reflect Your light
Ever waxing.

The Prayer Of The Poor In Will

Sometime in the early 1960s, I found myself filled with feelings of yearning for the presence of God in my life for which I did not have an expression. Then, one day, both the Hebrew and English of this prayer arose in me and I wrote it down. The acrostic is the English letters for the Divine names of God.

Yah gracious One, do hear my voice,
Despite my tumult's churning;
Though often I forget Thy joys,
Do mark my present yearning.

Help, do again dwell in my soul,
Despite my blind resistance,
To make Thee aim of every goal,
To sanctify existence.

Wouldst Thou Beloved draw me in,
Thy Being is my yearning;
Vain noises, sense-created din
Drown out mine inner turning.

How often did I wound Thine Heart?
Do show me how to free Thee,
How from my selfish sin to part,
How cease to ever mar Thee.

A house I cannot build for Thee;
Would that I still my tensions,
Would that my split will's enmity
Not change my soul's intentions.

Dry eyed, my heart unmoved remains,
Despite my abject flailings,
Turn – Thou who penitents sustain –
To merit all my failings.

Now in the fingers of my hand
I hold my will extended.
Take this poor gift while yet I stand,
Made thine, return it mended.

I turn to You, my blessed God,
That You take hold of this turning
And bring me home to be with You,
The goal of my soul's yearning.

September 11:
Prayer for Peace

This prayer was offered at a community service the evening after the attack on the United States.

May the Holy One who blessed our ancestors
and us over these many centuries,
helping us to get through the many tragedies
and the great pain we have known,
bless all those whose lives
have been changed by this violence.
May those who witnessed these events
find reconciliation and an inner peace
which allows them to live without fear.
May those who suffered injury
find healing and recovery.
And may those who have lost loved ones
find comfort and consolation
in the presence of family, friends, and community.

Our Mother, who is the source of our very being,
please gather the souls of those who passed on
in this tragedy under Your wings
and close to Your heart.
Keep them close to us who live on,
that they inspire us to seek peace,
to be peace, and to end the curse of killing,
hatred, and fear which blocks us
from becoming the compassionate beings
which You created us to be.

May the souls of those who were lost today
be bound up with those who live on
that we not forget the love they shared
and the love we all need to share.
May they rest in peace.
Amen.

Invocation Before the Sacred Union

From the writings of Rabbi Yossef Hayyim of Baghdad[34] author of *Ben Ish Ḥai*. He offered this prayer as a parallel to the most powerful *Ana B'khoaḥ*[35] attributed to Rabbi Neḥunia ben Haqqaneh. It is contained in his teachings concerning the blessing over blossoming fruit trees during the month of *Nissan*. I sense from the text that it was also meant to be recited before the holy mating.

Oh, that the beautiful Presence,
in endless compassion, shed Light all radiant!

Oh, that Your Will, God Most Exalted
in sound and inflection encoded, manifest in us!

Oh, that the mating most total and sacred
in infinite greatness, attain to the crowning!

We sprang from the Light-drop
in the womb of the Tzaddik, to grow to completion.

We entreat in this prayer the hope of our people,
that the blissful fulfillment send us its blessing.

Oh, that the mating most holy, most sacred,
be roused to its peak-point, as all power is sweetened!

May the root of the Tzaddik, the Way of the Sacred,
find its completion, right here and right now!

Through Time and Space Your glory shines, Majestic One.

---

34   Yossef Ḥayim (1 September 1832-30 August 1909) was a leading *Ḥakham* (Sephardic Rabbi), authority on Jewish law (*Halakha*) and Master Kabbalist. He is best known as author of the work on *Halakha, Ben Ish Ḥai* ("Son of Man (who) Lives"), by which title he is also known.
35   Page 41

Prayer Before *Havdalah*[36]

Gott fuhn Avrohom
A Yiddish prayer attributed to R'Levi Yitzḥak of Berditchev[37]

God of Avraham, Yitzḥak and Ya'akov
The Shabbat Kodesh is about to leave.
Protect us, Israel, Your dear folk, from all evil,
And keep us near to You in joy and praise.

The week is coming.
May it bring us:
to a faith, wholesome and complete,
to trust in the guidance of those who are aware,
to love for our companions,
to be attached only to you, our Creator,
to believe and live in your thirteen *Ikkarim* dimensions –
in our redemption of being near,
in the raising of the dead,
and in *Moshe Rabbenu's* vision of Truth.

Ribbono shel Olam – Cosmic Master –
You are the source of strength.
Infuse also with strength
Us, your *yiddishe kinderlakh*,
so we can praise You,
so we can serve You.
What more do we want?

---

36   *Havdalah* (lit., separation) is the ceremony on Saturday nights that separates the Sabbath from the rest of the week. It is made over wine, sweet smelling incense, and fire from a multi-wicked candle.

37   Rabbi Levi Yitzḥak of Berditchev (1740-1809), also known as the Berdichever, was one of the main disciples of the *Maggid* of Mezritch. He is known as one of the great intercessors of Israel.

Let the week bring health and mazal
success and grace, good children,
a decent livelihood,
For us, for all Israel –
AMEN!

Civic Prayers

"And work ye for the welfare of the city into which I have
deported you and pray on her behalf to Yah; for as she will
prosper, so will you." (Jeremiah 29:7)

We pray for things we care about. Somehow we
neglect to pray for a better quality of our social
environment. We are prepared to vote for a bet-
ter government, but we feel awkward about praying for it. That
uneasy attitude made sense at one time. In the past, it was part of
the Shabbat service to invoke God's help for the Czar, the Queen,
the Kaiser, or the Sultan. I have many a siddur and holy day prayer
book that has these patriotic gestures after the Torah reading on
the Shabbat. I suppose people felt even more awkward about praying for their rulers after the First World War; as if in a democracy
one need not bother to pose in what appeared to be an empty gesture meant to flatter one's "beloved Sovereign." They no longer
had to appease the Czar, may he live—far away from us.[38] Or imagine some people in a ḥavurah[39] praying for the President in the days
of Nixon.

I once attended a Native American peyote service in New Mex-
ico in which the Road Chief led in prayer and prayed for the President—it was Nixon then—and after I suppressed the first tremor of
a giggle, I really heard what was being offered:

Dear God, this man in the White House, he is responsible
for so many lives. If he thinks wrong, we are all in trouble.
Guide him, God, to feel good and to think right and to do
for this country what is right, so that all of us - the two

---

38   Reference to Fiddler on the Roof

39   Literally Fellowship. Ḥavurot are non-affiliated prayer groups that
meet on Shabbat and Holy Days. Reb Zalman was one of the founders of the
first one — Ḥavurat Shalom, Somerville, Mass. in 1968.

legged, the four legged, the winged and all our relations –
will be able to live and prosper.

So in this time of transition, I would like us to pray for
this under-prayed country and planet, and I invite you to
compose and recite prayers and to share them with others.
We need to think of this not as the patriotism of the past,
but the 'matriotism'[40] of our life system.

For the President – (give the name here) – and for his/her
Cabinet, we pray that they be guided to function at the
level of their highest ideals, fulfilling their promises, and
responding to the outcry of those who called them:

We pray ANA YAH!
For the welfare of this state and city:
We pray ANA YAH!
For the healing of family life:
We pray ANA YAH!
For the Healing of our Mother, the Earth:
We pray ANA YAH!
For the homeless and the hungry, the oppressed of the world:

We pray ANA YAH!

Term coined by Susan Saxe

V

Thank You Prayers

A Thank You Prayer

Thank You, God of Eternity,
for the great wonder of Your creation,
for the earth, the stars, the sun and the moon,
and the beauty of Your universe,
with which in Your great kindness You have blessed me.
Thank You for granting me life, in all its richness,
for its brilliant moments of joy,
which allow me to soar as the birds,
and even for its anguish and pain,
which somehow seem to precipitate inner growth and change.
For all these things, God, I am grateful.

But thank You, especially, God, in Your abundant love,
for having chosen to make me a human being,
blessed, among all the fruits of Your creation,
with a mind to reason and seek truth and justice;
with a soul which can feel pain, ecstasy, and compassion,
and has the freedom to choose life and goodness
over cruelty and destruction;
and with a heart which can love and care,
and reach out to touch the hearts of my brothers and sisters,
as together we walk through the years of our lives.

Al Hanissim
For the Miracles

l Hanissim—'for the miracles'—is a prayer that is inserted into the daily prayer services and in the Grace after Meals during the days of Ḥanukah. I was not too happy about the way in which all of Greek culture was considered wicked and evil so instead of mentioning the collective, I substituted King Antiokhus (c. 215 B.C.E.–163 B.C.E.) who, in his arrogance, considered himself to be Epiphanes – God manifest – and whose detractors called him Epimanes—'the madman'; he was the real villain of the Ḥanukah story. I changed the wording of the Thanksgiving insertion to be closer to the way in which we celebrate Ḥanukah today.

In the days of Matitiyahu
The High Priest and his sons,
When they were oppressed by
The reign of the wicked Tyrant Antiokhus
Who sought to uproot
Our faith and law
Pressing us to turn to idolatry,
His soldiers conquered our Temple
And desecrated our sanctuary.
Then Your devout priests
Arose against them,
And You in Your great compassion
Stood by them in their troubles,
Waging their wars,
Avenging their pain,
Helping them to overcome their enemies
And to purify the sanctuary.
Amidst longing for Your Presence
Among them,

They sought to kindle
The pure lamps
And not finding enough pure oil
You led them to find some
Just enough for one day.
In trust in Your caring
They kindled the sacred Lamp
And You, miraculously,
Made the oil last
Until they could make some afresh.
To celebrate your help and deliverance
They set these days of Ḥanukah
To become the feast
By lighting candles and by chanting
The Hallel in gratitude
To Your great reputation,
For Your miracles,
Your wonders,
And Your salvation.
They also encouraged us
To give Tzedakah to the poor
And toys to the children.

Thanksgiving

I have attended a number of Thanksgiving meals where more attention was paid to the turkey than to the attitude of gratitude. In our tradition, we have included in the *Birkat Hamazon* – the Grace after Meals—as well as in the *Amidah* prayer, a paragraph that celebrates our gratitude for Ḥanukah and Purim. Here I offer a Thanksgiving for the *Minḥa* prayer said in the afternoon before the Thanksgiving dinner and the *Birkat Hamazon* said after the meal. It has been my custom to sing the Psalm which introduces the *Birkat Hamazon* to the melody of the Thanksgiving hymn and to sing that hymn during the dinner.

For all the boons in our lives we offer our thanks to you
YHVH our God and in blessing your Name we hope that
all of life will bless You too and especially today because:

In the days of the Pilgrims, the Puritans, when they
arrived at these safe shores, suffered hunger and cold.
They sang and prayed to the Rock of their Salvation.
And You, standing by them, roused the caring of the
Natives for them: who fed them, turkey and corn and
other delights. Thus You saved them from starvation,
and they learned the ways of peace with the inhabitants
of the land. Therefore, feeling grateful, they dedicated
a day of Thanksgiving each year as a remembrance for
future generations, feeding unfortunates feasts of thanks.
Thus do we thank You for all the good in our lives, God of
kindness, Lord of Peace; thus do we thank You.

We gather together
to ask the Lord's blessing;
He chastens and hastens
His will to make known.

The wicked oppressing
now cease from distressing.
Sing praises to his name,
He forgets not his own.

Beside us to guide us,
our God with us joining,
ordaining, maintaining
His kingdom divine;
so from the beginning
the fight we were winning;
Thou, Lord, wast at our side,
all glory be Thine!

We all do extol thee,
Thou leader triumphant,
and pray that Thou still
our Defender wilt be.
Let thy congregation
escape tribulation;
Thy Name be ever praised!
O Lord, make us free!

Hannah's Canticle of Thanksgiving from 1st Samuel 2

Hannah prayed in her heart;
when she used words, she said:

My heart is ecstatic in Yah.
I now can hold my head high
because of You, Yah.
I now find words
to answer my rivals.
I jubilate because of Your help to me.

None is as holy as You, Yah.
No thing else besides You has being,
no bulwark keeping me as safe
as You do – our God.

Arrogant ones! Don't boast.
Let no gloating pour out from you.
Yah is the God of all awareness;
all plots are known to Him.

The weapons of the bullies
are made harmless
while those who faltered
were imbued with strength.

Those who were smug
are now starving.
The ones who were starving
are hungry no longer.
The one who seemed barren
gave birth to seven.
The prolific one is now in grief.

Yah kills and revives,
casts down into the pit
and raises one up.
It is Yah who makes some poor,
some rich,
humbles and ennobles,
lifting the down-and-out from the dirt.
The destitute one
He raises from the dunghill,
seating that one among
the power brokers,
offering her a seat of honor.

The very foundations of Earth
belong to Yah;
upon these He set the world.

He protects the steps of His devout ones.
The wicked hunker in dark silence.
Not with brutality does a man prevail.

Yah! His attackers are shattered.
Yah thunders in the sky.
He determines what happens
to the ends of the Earth.
He empowers his chosen king
and anoints him to excellence.

Hannah's Prayer

Along time ago, I was given a vinyl recording—"Women Of The Old Testament." As I listened to it, I came across this prayer. The lines in regular type were in the major key that fits the *halakhic* (legalistic) chant of the *Mishnah*, best known from when we sing the *Mah Nishtanah* – the four questions—at the Passover Seder. The italic lines were in the minor mode in which *Aggadic* (Talmudic sacred tales) are chanted. I knew right away that the composer must have been someone well acquainted with our traditions and melodies. The recording artist was listed as one Sarah Hirschfield.

A few years later, I was in Los Angeles as a scholar-in-residence. I had just recorded the "Tale of the Seven Beggars" of Rabbi Naḥman of Bratzlav and was busy selling the albums. A lady came over, examined one and asked me to sign it. I asked her name and she told me it was Sarah Hirschfield. I started to chant the first two lines of her recording, and she chanted the next two lines and we hugged. I still love to use this chant from time to time, which I believe she called: "I Will Sing unto the Lord."

I will sing unto the Lord
for all the joys He gave to me.
And I will weep unto the Lord
for those who have not shared in this joy.

I will sing unto my God
for all the Grace She poured on me.
And I will weep unto my God
for those who have not tasted of Her Grace.

I will sing unto the Lord
for all light He gave to me.
And I will weep unto the Lord
for those who did not get to share this blessed light.

I will sing unto my God
for all friends who share with me.
And I will weep onto the my God
for those who have no friend.

I will sing unto my God
for every quiet hour of peace.
And I will weep unto my God
for all who yearn for peace.

And I will weep
and I will sing
and I will sing with tears.

Thanks for the Food and Its Nourishment

he following three sections are taken from the *Birkat Hamazon* – the Grace after Meals – prayer. It is a good practice to regularly express gratitude and thanks for our food, nourishment and sustenance.

Praise, yes, praise is Yours, O God,
Ruler of all time and space,
Who every day invites the world
To the feast of love, goodness and compassion:
You feed us – and we earned it not;
You sustain us – and we deserved it not.

You so abundantly overwhelm us with
Your Goodness.
Food you provide for all Your creatures,
Whom You love so abundantly.

And because you are so good to us,
We have never lacked sustenance in the past,
And we believe that we will never lack food
In the future.

This You do for Your own repute
That You may be known as:
The one who sustains,
The One who supports,
The one who provides food for each
creature's needs.

For Your feast is prepared for all,
And Your table is set for all;
You know well what each one needs,
For You did create all.

Therefore do we praise and thank You,
The One who nourishes all.

We Remember Others
as We Remember Jerusalem.

We eat and drink
Yet we forget not that
There is exile, destruction,
Famine, fear and want.
Please, forget us not,
But in remembering us,
Remember all in want.
Make this world
A place of holiness,
Now in our lifetime,
As you rebuild Jerusalem.
Praised are you, O God,
Who in building up mercy
Builds Jerusalem.
Amen – do as we believe!

We Thank You For All
That You Are To Us.

Praise, yea praise to You, O God,
Source of our being
Merciful Mother
Mighty Father
Powerful Ruler
Redeeming Creator
Holy Artist
Jacob's Sanctifier
Guiding Shepherd
Israel's Shepherd
Sovereign who is good to all.

In Your goodness you do not discriminate,
doing good day by day according to that day's needs.

So You did act out of goodness in the past,
and so will You deal with us in the future.

You give of Your Self,
You gave of your Self,
You will give of Your Self
freely and completely
kindly and mercifully
generously and abundantly

to save us
to prosper us
to bless us
to redeem us
to console us
to sustain and support us —

in mercy, life, and goodness
while not diminishing
the good You hold in store for us for eternity.

VI

Songs of the Rabbis

The Song of the *Besht*

here was a time when I was teaching young people about the Ḥasidic masters, and I would also teach them some of the deeper Ḥasidic *niggunim* (wordless chants). But I saw that while people were singing them they had no idea of the conscious content that Ḥasidim summon up when chanting these melodies. At first, I explained to them what the conscious content was, but then I decided to set words to these melodies that would correspond to the feelings with which I was singing them. Later, I presented these to the late Lubavitcher Rebbe, Rabbi Menaḥem Mendel Schneersohn, and he approved them.

This text accompanies the *niggun* believed to come from the Ba'al Shem Tov[41] himself. It is sung in the order of AA BB CC BB and repeated CC and BB. CC soars high with longing.

As I sit and I sing,
I remember my heavenly home.
As I sit and I think,
I feel the nearness of God's throne.
Lord, my light, heart's delight,
Thee I seek, Thee alone.

Thy sweet Love, O God above,
Thrills me, fills me, gives me life,
With Thy Power, my Rock and Tower,
Thy Will to do I'll strive!

The rays of Grace Thy Torah radiates,
Guide me on the road to Thy heavenly abode.
Thy wisdom bright, understanding's light,
In knowledge will abide.
Oh Lord, lift my earthly load;

41   Rabbi Yisroel (Israel) ben Eliezer (August 27, 1698 — May 22, 1760), known as the Baal Shem Tov (Master of the Good Name) or the Besht, was a Jewish mystical rabbi and the founder of Ḥasidic Judaism.

Guide me on the road to Thy heavenly abode.
Thy wisdom bright, understanding's light,
In knowledge will abide.

Thy sweet love, O God above,
Thrills me, fills me, gives me life.
With Thy Power, my Rock and Tower,
Thy Will to do I'll strive!

The Rebbe's Song from the Rostov on the Don[42]

This *niggun*, known as the 'preparation *niggun*' was usually sung before the Rebbe began the special discourse on the Torah called the *ma'amar*. It allowed both the Rebbe and the Ḥasidim to create a circuit in which inspiration would come through the Rebbe.

> For the sake of my soul I search for a goal,
> And I find none other than Thee, O Lord.
> Thou findst satisfaction in our mitzvah action,
> If Thy light in Thy Torah we see.

> O grant me the awareness of Thy so precious nearness;
> In Thy presence, O Lord, I long to dwell.
> Help me from the start to make pure my heart,
> And all in the end will be well.

> O Lord so many years have gone by in great waste
> Till of Thy wondrous sweetness Thou has granted me a taste,
> Reach me please and teach me and keep me in thy Grace
> Until the day in which I may see Thy Holy face.

---

42   After Rabbi Shalom Dov Ber of Lubavitch was forced to flee Lubavitch during the First World War he settled in Rostov on the Don.

Words of Reb Yosef Yitzḥak to
the Melody of Reb Mikheleh

Rabbi Yosef Yitzḥak Schneersohn, my late Rebbe, left us a teaching—"I have come to my Garden"—before his passing.[43] He revealed that if we were to study it, he would be with us in prayer and intercede on our behalf.

Although you cannot be privy to it via the written text, I need to let you know that there is a *niggun* (melody) known as Reb Mikheleh Zlotchover's[44] *'Niggun of Longing'*. When Reb Mikheleh was a young man, his father travelled to visit the Ba'al Shem Tov. When he returned, Reb Mikheleh noticed his father's elevated inspiration. He begged his father to take him to meet this man. His father said: "I know that you want to meet the Ba'al Shem Tov, but we have to make sure that the Ba'al Shem Tov wants to meet you at this time." Out of intense longing, the young Mikheleh composed the first part of the *niggun*. When his father told him that on the next journey he would take him along, in anticipation, he composed the second part. After the visit, when he had to leave, he composed the third part of the melody.

When the Ba'al Shem Tov was preparing to die, he asked his disciples to sing this *niggun* and promised them that whenever they needed to have someone join them in prayer, if they were to sing this melody he would become their prayer partner.

Thus I combined Reb Mikheleh's melody with the gist of Reb Yosef Yitzḥak's teaching. Here are the words.

---

43   Reb Zalman recalls that on Friday Jan. 27th 1950 while working as a congregational rabbi in Fall River, Mass. he received the regular weekly *ma'amar* from the Rebbe. That Sabbath morning he and the other Ḥabad emissaries studied the text together. In the evening, after Sabbath had ended, they learned of the passing of their teacher and guide.
44   Yeḥiel Mikheleh of Zlotchov, 1731-1786

I came to my garden
From beyond time and space,
To meet my bride, my beloved,
At our special meeting place,
For not the angels of heaven above,
But you, my souls, I love.

My Lord, My Love, My Groom,
With Thee let me commune.
Please regard
That in my heart
For Thee I have made a room.

My Lord, My Love, My Groom,
Please save me from doom.
I shall heed
Thy word in deed
In joy but never in gloom.

Save my soul from evil's rule;
It makes one act just like a fool,
So that the truth I'll realize
And follow Thee, Oh Eternally wise.

To see then clear, just how ideal
It is for me, Thee near to feel,
So hear my Lord, do hear my sigh –
With Torah, Turning, and Right acts,
To Thee my knot I tie.

Naḥmania

Friends called me to submit a poem for a *Festschrift* for Allen Ginsberg, and this was the result.

Dear Rebbe,
dear Friend,
dear forerunner – barrier-breaker
enterer into brand new territories of God spaces;
Dear model *mensch* Jew,
menorah of countless flaws that sparkle
in their brilliance of God's Crown;
Dear Soul Romantic,
God lover,
poet *zaddik* –
leviathan playmate of the infinite;
dear childholiness,
dear old rake rogue, you knew
of those matings of souls that last
from seconds, to hours and weeks, months, years or lifetimes.
You died too young to play it all out,
but you sure had all the makings,
whose hassidim study his Torahs, stories,
sing his songs and dance his dances
– but, alas, don't laugh with him,
nor know when he is joking
and don't quite dig the drama of him
sitting and playing chess with *T'refe possul* of the town,
appreciating their guts
while at the very same time
also digging R' Nossen's ride
as the perfect ḥassid
of the perfect Rebbe,
I want to tell you that I know you,

dig and *grok* some few of your fantastically many facets,
including your scheme
for putting a neat elegant finale on history,
I love and honor you; I salute you,
Reb Naḥman of Bratzlav.

You knew from outdoors,
from meditating in boats and letting them just float,
taking a ride on God's back;
from riding a horse into the forest and then
getting so spaced out that you and the horse came back
different times and ways.

You so grabbed for your transformations each day –
What? You be the same two days in a row?
You had to be Reb Naḥman
the very unique and identifiable Naḥman,
the genius consciousness artist,
doing every role in every play,
convincingly, brilliantly,
yet with the signature of your insight clearly visible;
I applaud you.

GEVAAAAAALT!
"You are still afraid of the curtain?
Come on, Zalman! When one
curtain falls another one goes up.
Don't you know it really
lasts as long as God will dream
you so you might as well do it
all in style. So DON'T DESPAIR!"
"Remember," you ask me, "the teaching that I said: '
they tell us
that there is a this world
and an other world and a hell, – and

that I said we were all in hell,
but in order to make it a
little easier on us they tell us we are in this world.'"

Yes, I remember. Now you think differently –
we are really in Paradise,
but we like to go, see good
and convincing heavy movies.
Even in the comedies
they have routines of death and dying.
So you advise me every day
to practice the suspension of "the suspension of disbelief,"
and look around and really see
that we are not even on the set,
that we are just watching the movie.

Yes, it is heavy to wake up to an alarm clock,
but we set it so it should
wake us up in time.

VII

An Assortment

The Prayer Of A Monist

The mind enjoys reaching towards unity. It can conceptually reach to infinity in solitude. On the other hand, the heart needs to flow to a dialogical Presence. It needs to have the Other to face and to love and to embrace. The contemplative, who still wants to experience love and longing without relinquishing the unitive awareness will find this poem a heart-full expression of what the intellect knows and the soul intuits. (The oneness of the individual person and the divine person I have tried to express in the acrostic in which the personal, my name—MeSHuLaM ZaLMaN—is embraced by the two Divine names Y-H-V-H and EHYH. Similar patterns can be found in other religious poetry, as in the great Reb Aaron Karliner's *Yah Ekhsof* in the original Hebrew.)

Yah, my God, where are You?
I call You as if from afar
and You Redeemer, dwell in my heart —
so close and I know it not.
Here You are, present in my innermost,
and so, too, are You at the outermost edge —
both Source of mine and goal!
Where my feelings rise in me,
there are You stirring me, nesting in the womb of my urge.

Here in my eye's pupil are You,
and I yearn so much to make
You object of my sight.
My innards would become - if only pure,
how I would scour them - Your sanctuary in me
made sacred by Your Presence.
Show me how to host You,
What a blessing! Your nestling in my heart.

Life of my life, You are within me,
so how could I meet You
on the outside?
My song would be addressed to You
were You beside me
and not hidden in my voice.
Zoned in the point of knowing,
You hide in unseen splendor —
glorious as I seek Your Glory.
Lingering on Your threshold,
my ego squats, claiming to be
the legal tenant of Your home.
More I cannot confuse the two
who shimmer as one I-AM-ness.
Never can I leave this labyrinth, my self
by myself.
Do help me sortie and free me.
Then my pray'r will be pure for You.
Echo — are You the call or the answer?
Even these words, are they mine
or Yours?
Help and tell me, Love of my Heart.
Are You not also
the Love and the Heart?
Yah! God, adored One,
I want to offer You
a gift You will not spurn, Your will be mine.
Is it not already so?
Holy solitude, All One Al-one,
my sole One,
My soul's One, my part(ner)
My wholly—Holy Other—One.
AMEN

Dirge on Auschwitz

This was written after the Holocaust (when Russian Jews were still oppressed in Soviet Union) and we were still reciting laments and dirges that came from Middle Ages. I felt I needed something that spoke to us in our time. This is the English version.[45]

Alas, how poor are words to state our pain
In remembering the millions slain,
While yet upon our souls the stain
Of standing by while brothers called in vain.

Unshriven here we are depressed
As long as somewhere someone is oppressed,
As long as the murderers the meek suppressed,
And grieving mothers wail distressed.

Shalt Thou, O God, not bear Thy guilt this day
For standing by while multitudes in blood do lay?
And silent Thou unmoved didst stay,
Thy covenant to help us didst betray.

While millions' lives to ash were turned,
To their last breath, they for Thine intervention yearned,
Still hoping day and night, while all the ovens burned.
Why were our prayers of desperation spurned?

If Thine own we are, O Lord, then Thou art King,
And if only by Thy leave occurs each thing,
Then butcher Thou, and we the offering.
Yet who, but Thou, can heal our suffering?

45   The Hebrew version can be found in *Paradigm Shift - From the Jewish Renewal Teachings* of Reb Zalman Schachter-Shalomi (Jason Aronson 2000). Note the acrostic that forms the Aus(h)wits.

The help Thou sendest must renew
All of mankind, not just the Jew,
The Arabs and the Russians, too,
Must be freed, ere peace is true.

Send Thine anointed Savior, Lord,
To turn to plowshare atom's sword.
May each in Him see One adored
And prophesied by prophet's word.

Graceful Passage

When I was approached to contribute to a recording[46] intended for people at the end of their life, I spoke these words not to the dying, but as if I myself were on my deathbed.

God, You made me.
From before I was born,
You took me through my life.
You supported me.
You were there with me when I wasn't there with You.
There were times I was sick and You healed me.
There were times I was in despair
and You gave me hope.
There were times when I felt betrayed,
and I could still turn to You.

It was a wonderful life. I loved and I was loved.
I sang, I heard music, I saw flowers,
I saw sunrises and sunsets.
Even in places when I was alone,
You, in my heart, helped me turn loneliness
into precious solitude.
I look back over the panorama of my life;
what a wonderful privilege this was!

I still have some concerns for people in the family,
for the world, for the planet.
I put them in Your Blessed Hands.

---

46   From the CD "Graceful Passages : A Companion for Living and Dying" by Gary Remal Malkin

I trust that whatever in the Web of Life
that needed me to be there
is now completed.
I thank You for taking the burden from me,
and I thank You for keeping me in the Light,
as I let go, and let go, and let go... and let go.

Source of Time and Space

Elias Amidon and his wife Rabia (Elizabeth Roberts), Sufi leaders active in peace work in the Middle East, have created a number of collections of prayers relevant to our current life. This is my contribution to their book, *Prayers for a Thousand Years.*[47]

Source of Time and Space –
Avinu Malkaynu!

From infinity draw down to us
The great renewal
And attune us to Your intent,
So that Wisdom, Your daughter,
Flows into our awareness,
To awaken us to see ahead,
So we help instead of harm.

May all the devices we make use of
Be sparing and protecting
Of Your creation.

Help us
To set right what we have debased,
To heal what we have made ill,
To care for and to restore
What we have injured.

Bless our Earth, our home,
And show us all
How to care for her,

47   *Prayers for a Thousand Years* by Elizabeth Roberts and Elias Amidon (HarperOne, 1999)

So that we might live
Your promise
Given to our forebears
"To live heavenly days
Right here on this Earth."

May all beings
Whom You have fashioned,
Become aware that it is You
Who has given them being.

May we realize that
You shaped our lives,
And may each one who breathes
Join with others who breathe
In the delight of shared knowing
Of the great breath.

Assist us in learning
How to partner
With family, neighbors,
And friends.
Aid us in dissolving old enmities.

May we come to honor,
Even in those whom we fear,
Your image and form, Your light
Dwelling in their hearts.

May we soon see the day, when
Your House will be indeed,
The House of prayer
For all peoples,
Named and celebrated
In every tongue and speech.
On that day You will be one
And one with all cosmic Life.
Amen!

A Meditation On The Primary Word

When I first read Martin Buber's *I and Thou*, I was greatly moved and wrote the following poem.

Ex. 14:3 "Said Pharaoh concerning the
Children of Israel: They are entangled
in'earth'ness; shut out to them is the Wilderness
(*Midbar* – power of speech)."

Ex. 14:14 "YHVH will battle for you
if you be without speech."

There are two primary words
I–THOU and I–IT.

Suddenly it dawns on me
We have never spoken I–THOU
We have never spoken I–IT.

O yes, we have said it many a time –
mouthed the words – formed them with our lips,
but we have never spoken them.
I wonder,
can they be spoken?
Can primary words ever be uttered,
pronounced by the means of that
which talks and talks and still cannot reveal?
Yet wherein lies the power of speech?
Not in the sound of the babbled,
the dumb sound of mouth's noise;
not in the rasp falling on the ear's diaphragm,
but in that which
"He does not say – there are no words;
without being heard is their voice."
The primary word has no sound,

yet only it has meaning.
The word which is
promise, oath, commitment
is not in what is heard.
Yet is it not perceived?
Did I not listen for it?
Have you not answered it?
I—AM—He said,
I – SHALL BE WHAT I SHALL BECOME!
So we bet our lives on it
and answered:
"We shall do and obey!"
(Not "we shall hear and decide.")
In becoming aware of the call,
we have long since decided.
This decision was the word of our response.

But why does it not last?
Why can I not keep it with me forever?
Because it exists
in eternity!
It was not heard with ears
nor uttered with mouth.
The uttered word comes after
the primary word,
and only the uttered word makes
sound
while the primary word is spoken
in silence.
Can I be aware of speaking
the primary word?
Can I be aware of hearing
the primary word?

Can I cut out the tongue
of the nightingale,
dissect it,
and hear its music?

I can only become aware that
it has been spoken –
never hear it at the moment when
the primary word is spoken.
For the primary word is a total word –
the blast of the ram's horn is
the primary word –
I - THOU it screams
in all tonalities,
past the confines of the conscious.

Yet from the unconscious alone
no primary word emerges.
There is no THOU
nor IT
in the unconscious.
In the conscious there are
many its,
many Thous reduced to its,
but no I - THOU
no I - IT.
In the unaware there are no concepts,
in the aware only concepts
but in the Person,
the whole – undivided Person,
the full and complete Person,
the really present Person
in the immanence of the awareness,
in the transcendence of the unaware –
when both are fused,
there emerges
the primary word.

Pharaoh needs labels:
"Who is YHVH
that I shall heed
His voice?"
Moses cannot tell him

166 Rabbi Zalman Schachter-Shalomi

how to conceptualize
relation.
The slavish hordes
which are Israel–to-be,
cannot conceptualize relation.

YHVH has sent me
to relate His – I—AM
to YOU
EHYH—I SHALL BE.
What I shall be
without deadening arrest
in the present
which a moment from now
will be ....past
will be concept—label—empty word
EHYH—I SHALL BE
EXISTENT
Ever Present ....YHVH
I who make the present
exist.

Man—THOU art
Person,
child, friend, person,
so like My Self,
part of My Self,
yet self in your own right.
I AM I
not because you are you.
You are You
not because I Am I;
But I being I
and YOU being YOU
can relate
freely
never grabbed—arrested by labels –
never bound by concepts.

I Am – without strings attached;
You Are—as you are.

ANOKHY—I AM.
I give my I am to You.
I have not given,
I do not say I shall give,
I give
my unnamed unnamable
ineffable self
ANOKHY
to You.
This is the first
Commandment,
which still rings
through the ages,
which frees from bondage,
which at-ones for the present,
which gives the law
for relation:

Thou shalt not make thee
a graven image,
a concept . . .

Do not put my name
on anything which is
vanity,
for how can I cleanse,
at-one, free,
for the one who makes my I
a concept?

Be reasonable, work,
conceptualize, make tools
of things of Its
six days a week.
I do not demand

(What can you give Me?
What needs can you fill in Me?
For needs are filled by
objects – things – concepts,
yet I am jealous
that you must let me be
what I AM
and not a concept.)
I love freely,
to relate to thousands of generations,
so remember,
keep one day free
to be with me,
as I am as You are
I - THOU
in a state of primary existence,
primary, unsullied, free from taint
of concepts,
as it was when
I THOU, God Adam
Related – before you wanted to
know-conceptualize . . .
just once a week to live
eternity.

How can you learn to relate?
Honor!
Thy father and thy mother
as persons,
so that your days may be lengthened,
not shortened, driven, rushed
by concepts –

Do not murder person
by killing what is alive
transcending concept.
Do not whore
after love and relation;

do not use person
as if person was a thing.
What you have not earned
by relating,
do not – abstract –
steal.
Do not answer to your
friend
a false witness,
transference, carryover
of your conceptualization
belonging to other persons,
to your friend.
But most of all do not brood,
heatedly wallow,
in the mire of concepts,
the mud of the dreary,
wish-thinking
of unreality.

How sick am I,
having heard and yet remained deaf
to His Voice.
Was it deliberate that I mixed
the primary words?
Used I - IT when I - THOU
was indicated . . . .?
Claimed I- THOUNESS to my
possessions -
things concepts feces dirt
only to make from it
I – I I – ME I – MINE?

Suddenly it dawns on me –
I have never spoken,
I — THOU,

in all my wretchedness
I find no way to utter
the primary word except
amidst sobs my soul has said,
I — THOU.
Happy are the people
knowing TERUAH

O Lord in the Light of Thy innermost
they shall walk

Blessed art Thou . . . .

Dawn

My custom, whenever I spend some time in Israel is to take an all night vigil at the Holy Wall in the Holy city of Jerusalem. In the morning I like to go up the stairs to watch the sun rise as I pray. Remarkably, the prayers of the people at the wall are accompanied by the sound of the *Muezzin* call the faithful to prayer. It was such a morning that inspired me to write these lines.

Each day another version of the dawn.
Gentle pink blushes
color the blanching horizon
and billow-pillows softly promise
to receive the rising sun.

Lo, this quiet hour when the day begins
to break forth
from the fetters of the night
and stretches arms across the sky
and with pink floods yawns aloud.

And in the hearts of those whose eyes
have witnessed miracle
so common yet so new
a joyous hope makes its debut,
each day again as ne'er before.

Now if you pray, my friend, do join
the ranks of Yogis in *surya namaskar*
and betallissed Jew
or celebrant who greets the sun
with *dominus vobiscum*.

And then at last the sun appears
and over silhouetted horizon peers
with golden blinding ray
does kiss your soul and
melts the last hard lump not solved by night and rest.

Yes bring on, O day, what bring you must
How can I this day forsake this trust
Which dawn again has kindled in this breast
HOLY LORD AMONG YOUR ANGELS I LIKE DAWN THE BEST.

Der Geyer
The Walker

By Menahem Boraisha

*D*er Geyer (The Walker) is a panoramic epic, a *Bildungs-roman* in Yiddish verse. Written from September 1933 to June 1942, the dedication in the book reads: "to my children and their contemporaries."

Published in 1943 by Matones and reissued several times since (but never in English), the book is even taxing to the average Yiddish reader. Boraisha knew this, and in his notes explained many historical elements that he had used in the novel.

Der Geyer is Boraisha's crowning achievement. In it, he treats the themes he deals with in Zamd, Zavl Riemer (1923) and refines the poetic skill he exhibited in his *Ring un Keyt* and the epic form that entered into his *Der Gilgul* (1930) and *Pastukh Dovid. Der Geyer* won for Boraisha the Louis Lamed Fund Award. He died February 12, 1949. A modern heir to the writers of *Mussar* literature, he wedded Jewish moral thought to the poetic muses.

It takes a literature several generations to produce a writer of such scope and skill. With the exception of A.M. Klein, no one has done for Anglo-Jewish letters what Boraisha did for Yiddish.

Boraisha, born 1888 in Brest-Litowsk, was first known as Menaḥem Goldberg. His father Noah Goldberg, a *haskalah* Hebrew teacher, could have served Boraisha as a model. The insights portrayed are, however, autobiographical.

Noah, the hero, experiences the life of many a Jewish intellectual. It takes him through *ḥeder* and *yeshivah* to an early marriage, to confrontations with the new and the old, and to tense relations with the establishment. He is not a reformer. He is a contemplative. He wonders about Good and Evil. In order to earn a living that will allow him to think, he becomes a night watchman in the forest. Many of the images, as will be seen below, are taken from the creatures encountered in the night of the forest.

I translated these two fragments in 1964, trying to keep the
tempo and rhyme of the original, while teaching Yiddish at the Uni-
versity of Manitoba. The first is a brilliant meditation on the inner
voices that incessantly chat away in the mind. The image portrayed
by Lilith is, in my opinion, one of the most brilliant renditions of the
shadow side in all of literature. The second piece brings to life, in a
wonderful display of Yiddish humor, the now-extinct shtetl. I offer
it to the reader as a dim reflection of Boraisha's original, and I hope
that someone better endowed as a translator than I will one day offer us a complete translation of *Der Geyer*.

A Dark Night's Meditation

In your mind there sits a mother,
The pious mother – your Jewish faith.
She trembles in anguish
Lest you think *shegetz* thoughts.
To pacify her – divert her –
You set up a Purim play,
Put words into the maws of beasts,
And, like Balaam's Ass,
They argue.

THE CROW
As love binds you here below
To the dog at your feet,
So in heaven God is bound
To Satan at His feet,
The dog is robber, killer, hunter,
But to you he is a slave.
Do not seek to change him, cure him;
His fate tells him be a brave.

So your kindly God in heaven
Keeps old Satan next to Him.
Satan-death and Satan-evil
Nuzzles close to source of light.

ANOTHER CROW
When they both love one another,
One cannot be without the other.

THE BAT
Dusk is good, a decent time.
Light and dark mix in this clime.
Embrace and kiss heav'n 'n' hell.
All love flows freely from their well.
No one likes the brilliant day.
Blind at night fills with dismay.
Blinded, blind. Who cares which one?
Blind at night. Blinded by sun!
But dusk desired is by all.
Pretenses slip away and fall,
And desires are unmasked.
The truth the world speaks, unasked.
Day gives glow and night a wing,
Golden outline, bluish veil
Wrapped in dark. Limned in shimmer
Then she's truly the world;
Then we know her fully.

HAWK
Crow in dogs her simile seeks.
Bat finds hers in darkness.
Those who seek the dusk for ease
Fear the truth of starkness.
Not a dog, a wolf is Satan,
Wolf with sharpened fangs,
To kill and maim and mock
God's creation's ranks.
That which keeps one to the other
Is not love, is hate instead.
With the ring of creating-killing
Eternity holds them married, wed.

FOX
And the law of love's compassion
Invented have the weak ones. Mice,
In holes and rabbits anxious,
Beg for mercy, ask, "Be nice."

SWALLOW
Two imperatives are given
All obey them, angel, clod.
One from Satan comes persisting?
And the other comes from God.

HAWK
One for the chickens,
Another for the hawks.
If the hawk will eat,
Then the chicken squawks.
One is for the lambkins,
Another for the wolves.
When they attack and yelp,
Lambkin cries out: "Help!"
Lambs and chickens, they all cry,
All the way to Mt. Sinai.
Where is your mercy, Lord?
And the glutton Moloch
Mocks: Kill on lads! Enjoy
The gifts of my board.

RABBIT
But when the Ox of herbivores
The braggart wolf with his horns gores,
Old Moloch then
How he shall rue his lot!

SWALLOW
And when the storm comes with its zest
Carrying hawklets from their nest,
Ho! How love will prey exceed!
How for mercy you will plead!

BAT
The killer wings his way with booty
To his children's hungry mouth.
The victim screams and curses fate
And knows that no one hears its shout.
Love; without a little hatred,
Is a heart not caged by ribs.
Hatred without a little loving
Is a mouth with teeth, no lips.

PINYE'S VOICE
Animals with blind grey matter
Study *kamets*, aleph, OH.
We, the thinkers, we, the students,
Can begin with letter TOV.
We, the crown of all creation,
Sh'khinah's light in Adam's frame,
Do include all combinations
Of gender, name, and fame.

Wolves and lambs dwell in our innards;
Dove and hawk and spider-fly,
Brooding hatred sets apart,
Yet each kind heeds its own's outcry.
If we are life's highest level,
Still, we are the Form of God.
Is He not Himself the Devil?
Are they both not One – just God?
He, the Cossack with the knife,
He, the child that lost its life,
Creates and destroys with might
In a hurricane of black and white.
Who to whom antagonistic?
Wrestles He with Him Himself?
How can you bring peace to Him
If He is not at peace Himself?
Between light and darkness, always,
So revolving endlessly,

You in agony must suffer
A moment of eternity.
When this moment fades away,
And you return to naught again,
Then – yes, then – you know the answer,
Know your life was not in vain.

LILITH
All life comes
From Mother's womb,
In Eden's garden
There was no shame, no blame,
No guilt, no sin.
Until the fool, your ancestor,
The fruit of folly tasted.
He, then, God's wisdom wasted;
Now you bear the curse –
Of lust and fear, of love and shame.
And a Torah flays you
With a whip of blame.
The womb – incestuous vessel,
Womb – miracle of creation,
Heavenly joy,
Vain hell of pain;
Aspiring to the stars,
Animal's desires;
Union with God's Presence,
Cain's blind hatred;
Joy of the farthest generation,
Murderous exertion; all these
In that small span of life,
Which is the womb of wife.
This is how He wanted it,
So He made it thus –
That in this span of hidden life
Generations slumber,
And from menstruous fount
You draw your highs and lows,

Why to God a Devil tie
If pure, impure, is in your eye?
In you reside both joy and sigh.
Why should you clasp unto your hands
Countless rules and hard commands?
When holy joy and vile remorse
Both do issue from that source.
Why split and rip one from its mate
When the black and the white,
Like newlyweds' estate,
From Him alone, paired are the two?
In Him alone, paired are the two.
God did not want to separate
From your ancestor in Eden,
So he brought to him the sleeper
And mated him so he could see deeper.
Know the secret of creation:
Be a God yourself!

A voice issues from behind you;
You are not alone in anguish.
All are frightened, all do shiver.
The sounds of dogs and birds
Do show their hurts.
All shiver with you,
And in the shiver find
That they are your kind.

All sorts of poisonous thoughts
Like serpents wend their way in,
Entangling you in doubt.
Intoxicated by their brew,
With burnt tongues,
They crumble in dust,
– But a brother's calamity
Rouses you with pity.
When you consider him
Who burns in hell,

You don't measure his good, his evil.
You do not weigh his deeds.
You know him a sufferer
Like yourself,
And in his calamity,
Your heart knows pity.

Your fear, your anguish,
For each moment of life,
Reveals the matrix of eternity.
And in its calamity
Your heart knows pity.

A Ballad

A *shtetl* ("village"),
far from the highway,
the *shtetl* Jews, peasants,
do business with the village,
work for the farmers.
in his room, door locked,
the rabbi studies,
and the books on his shelves multiply.
He makes his way to town,
finds a holy book,
the seller names his price;
weeks of wages!
I'll be back,"
and the rabbi goes
to borrow the money.
In the morning he is back,
but too late;
the bookseller cuts him off.
It's sold. Some coachman bought it.
A coachman? A *baalagulah*,
a book of Kabbalah?!
The rabbi, not knowing
if the dealer teases,
walks into the slumstreets and asks for
the *baalegulah* who buys books.
They just stare at him.
The last one on his list
boards at the shoepatcher.
The rabbi gets his shoes patched.
He asks: "What is in these books you buy"
"Oh," the *baalegulah* replies,
"tales and stories."
The rabbi, his suspicions confirmed,

"Could have guessed as much.
Imagine, *baalegulahs* and Kabbalah!"
His heart brined in salt,
disgusted by the loss of the book,
and the bookseller's teasing,
he wants only to travel home.
He goes to the market to find a ride.
"Ready to go," the *baalegulah* yells
"Hop in, let's move!"
Amazed, the rabbi wonders,
only one fare and he travels?
"Come up, rabbi, don't worry!"
The *baalegulah* high on the driver's seat,
the rabbi under the covered wagon's hood,
they travel.

Only an hour or two, he thinks,
and I'll be home.
But soon he feels a halt
and looking out
he hears the *baalegulah* say:
"Come! Crawl out and look at this!"
The rabbi crawls, looks,
but cannot even recognize the road.
"Is this not a strange road?" he asks.
"It'll get to be your own. Look!"
And he points to a field,
peasants barefoot, scythes in hand, cutting hay:
Fragrant hay! Rolling fields! Vaulted sky!
Bird swarms swooping overhead!
"I see nothing," says the rabbi.
"O.K.! We'll keep on trucking!"
Hours pass, suddenly another stop.
"Come on out, rabbi!"
This time, even more alien,

a field and forest.
The *baalegulah* stops to chat
with a village peddler.
"Why drag me around?"
The rabbi is angry,
but the *baalegulah* just says,
"This fellow can use a ride; move over and we'll
take him a spell."
The wagon moves on,
the peddler and the rabbi
sitting under the hood.
The rabbi's silence breathes icy anger,
so the peddler keeps his peace
and they move on.
Another stop! Now its a *kuzhnya* ("smithy")
in some strange *shtetl*.
The peddler leaves, moving on his way.
The *baalegulah* waits in the *kuzhnya*
for the *kowal* ("smith") to shoe the horse.
He calls outside to the rabbi:
"Come on in, its happier here."
At the door of the smithy
stands the rabbi, growling with anger.
"What impertinence!
All I need is to overhear
the conversations
of *kowals* and *baalegulahs*!"

Finally, they travel on.
But soon oats are needed for the horse,
so on to the feedstore.
In friendly conversation stand
the storekeeper,
the *baalegulah* and a woman.
The rabbi burns with rage:

"When will there be an end to this!"
The *baalegulah* looks at him:
"It's a good store,
good folks here.
Why don't you come in?"
The rabbi bites his lip:
Even exile will someday find its end...
Night falls and they drive up
to a *kretchma* ("roadhouse").
As the *baalegulah* unhitches the horse,
the rabbi starts to go,
trying to find his colleague in the *Shtetl*.
But he is stopped:
"You'll find good people
in the roadhouse, too."
The ḥutzpah (audacity) of the *baalegulah*
Imprisons him and he stays.
The *kretchma* is filled with simple folk – eating, drinking, smoking.
He finds a corner and prays the *Ma'ariv* ("Evening Prayer").
He lets himself be served supper
while the *kretchmer* and the *baalegulah* hum.
Tired of his anger, he naps
and knows not when lamps are doused
and where the night got lost.
The day grays to dawn
and the *baalegulah* shakes him awake.
He wants to wash his hands for prayer.
But the other rushes him:
"You'll *daven* (pray) at home."
Now the wagon flies,
the road looks familiar.
The sun is fully up,
and they are at the rabbi's house.
"Rabbi! Arrived!"
Feeling fortunate, at home at last,

he reaches for his wallet.
"How much do I owe you?" he asks.
"You owe me nothing," the answer comes.
"I'll even pay you!"
And he pulls out the book
and gives it to the rabbi.
"Take it, rabbi.
If you see nothing
and hear nothing,
this book won't help you either!"
He turns to his horse
and urges him with a "Heigh-Ho!"
The rabbi stands there confused.
He rushes to pursue the wagon
but the *baalegulah* is way gone.

From his prison cell
Reb Shneur Zalman
addresses the Gaon of Vilna

Reb Shneur Zalman[48] and his senior colleague Reb Menaḥem Mendel of Vitebsk,[49] attempted to reach the Gaon of Vilna[50] for a personal encounter in order to demonstrate to him that Ḥasidism is not a heresy. The Gaon refused to see them. One of the results was that the persecution of the Ḥasidic movement increased and in 1798 Reb Shneur Zalman was arrested and imprisoned in the Petropavlovski fortress in St. Petersburg for fifty-three days, at which time he was subjected to an examination by a secret commission. Ultimately he was released by order of Paul I of Russia. Menaḥem Boraisha envisioned how Reb Shneur Zalman protested to the Gaon who at that time was no longer on this physical plane.

It is now the second time that the informers,
with the permission granted by your Ḥerem,
have brought me here.
The Holy One of Blessing released me the first time,
and He will save me again.
But you, Reb Elijah,
may the merit of your Torah protect you.

---

48   Rabbi Shneur Zalman of Liadi, also known as the Baal HaTanya (1745 – 1812), was founder and first Rebbe of Ḥabad, later known as the Lubavitch branch of Ḥasidism. He was recognized as the leader of the Ḥasidic movement in Lithuania at that time.

49   Rabbi Menaḥem Mendel of Vitebsk/Horodok (1730 – 1788) was an early leader of Ḥasidic Judaism. Part of the third generation of Ḥasidic leaders, he was the primary disciple of the Maggid of Mezeritch. From his base in Minsk, Menaḥem Mendel was instrumental in spreading Ḥasidism throughout Belarus.

50   Elijah ben Shlomo Zalman (1720 – 1797) known as the Vilna Gaon or Elijah of Vilna or simply by his Hebrew acronym The GRA ("Gaon Rabbenu Eliyahu") was a Talmudist, halakhist, kabbalist, and the foremost leader of non-Ḥasidic Jewry of the past few centuries.

Call Reb Mendel of Horodok.
He, too, is with you up there in the world of truth.
Ask him: What was it that we wanted
when we stood behind your door
with meekness and humility
and begged you to listen to our plea?

Empowered and encouraged
by your decree and reputation,
your emissaries traveled to many communities,
proclaiming that Ḥerem (excommunication)
and declaring the bread, the wine, and the daughters
of kosher Jews unfit, unkosher!
They declared their possessions free to be looted.
And the principal Satanic agent of defilement
with his scythe, cutting down and harvesting,
grabbing Jewish souls,
immersing them in sin and bloodlust,
goading them to ruthlessness and calumny,
denouncing us to a cruel and heartless government.
For two days we stood behind your door,
our weakened lips repeated the fervent prayer:
stop the destruction being wreaked on the house of Israel!
And you, not even gracing to look at us,
nor to listen to us,
fled the city.
May the merit of your Torah protect you.

And I, having written a small collection of sayings,
how a person might cleave to his Creator,
gathered it all in my little book,
and you allowed for this book to be burnt in public!
And again you send out your disciples,
from community to community,
to sow seeds of war, lawlessness, and murder.

Now you are already in the world of truth
(and know what the real truth is),
and still, your decree remains in force,
still potent to deliver Jewish souls drowned in sin
into the hands of the Prince of defilement
brutally spilling blood, libeling them.
May the merit of your Torah protect you.

If you saw me unworthy of the privilege
to debate with you in this world
– then – there, in the world of truth,
call my Rebbe Reb Ber for a dispute,
call the Baal Shem Tov, call the Ari,
call Rabbi Shimon ben Yohay, call the prophet Elijah,
call Moses our teacher – and let there be issued a decree –
(and I know that we disagree about this point)
if, as you say, only a dim and minor reflection of the Blessed
Infinity
poured itself into the *Sefirot*,
and that there is no possibility of purification and cleaving
to bring to the holiest of souls
more than a weak reflection,
then let your *Herem* hold in its legitimacy,
and in all submission we will accept deserved punishment.
But, if the Blessed Infinite One
shared His own light with the *Sefirot*,
and every soul is a drop of that light,
and the lowest person is capable of the purification and cleaving,
and can connect himself fully with the Holy Blessed Source –
way beyond every wisdom and comprehension –
then I ask you to appear to your heirs, your disciples,
let them know with an omen, a sign, what the decision was
so that the devastation of the House of Israel be stopped!

I'm not asking this because of my own suffering,
I'm not asking this for my reputation.
God has redeemed me once and will redeem me again
because even right here within the walls of the prison
Divine Providence hovers over me.
I'm only asking that there should be peace
for the house of Israel.
And even for your reputation in the other world.
I stand before the door of the prison cell,
just as then behind your door,
which you locked for me now as you locked your door then,
and I pray: may the *Shekhinah* have compassion on you
so that you no longer be the cause that destroys the peace!
May the merit of your Torah protect you.

VIII

The Songs of David[51]

---

51   There are 150 Psalms. Reb Zalman has translated almost all of them over the years. Here are his favorite seven.

Zug'n Tehillim, reciting the psalms, was once considered the prayer of last resort. Rabbi Pinḥas of Koretz[52] interpreted the verse (Psalm 106), "He who wishes to describe the power of the Lord, let him sound out all His praises," as a reminder to those needing to diminish the harsh decrees hanging over them to recite the entire Book of Psalms.

When the German general Rommel, the Desert Fox, was threatening to invade the Holy Land, it is said that there was an old woman in Jerusalem who urged the people: "Don't rely on miracles, recite the psalms!"

Psalm 23
A David Song

Yah, my shepherd, you supply my needs.
I don't ever feel deprived.

You feed me in the meadows.
I am led to quench my thirst by a quiet stream.

You stir my soul
And guide me gently
Through the thicket
Of right action;
Such is Your fame.

At times I must make my way
Through dark and dangerous gullies.
But because You are with me
I won't panic if I have to face evil.

---

52   Rabbi Pinḥas of Koretz (1728-1790), a famous Ḥasidic rebbe and one of the closest disciples of the Baal Shem Tov.

Both Your rebuke
And Your bracing support
Give me comfort.

In the presence of adversity
You set me a feast,
At which my anxious head is soothed
And my thirst is amply slaked.

Psalm 27
David's song

Yah, you are my Light, my Savior,
Whom need I dread?
Yah, with You as my strong Protector
Who can make me panic?
When hateful bullies gang up on me,
Wanting to harass me,
To oppress and terrorize me,
They are the ones
Who stumble and fall.

Even if a gang surrounds me
My heart is not weakened.
If a battle is joined around me
My trust in You is firm.
Only one thing do I ask of You, Yah,
Just this alone do I seek:
I want to be at home with You, Yah,
All the days of my life.
I want to delight in seeing You,
When I come to visit You
In Your Temple.

You hide me in Your *Succah*
On a foul day.
You conceal me unseen in Your tent
And also raise me beyond
Anyone's reach.
And now, as You have held
My head high,
Despite the presence
Of my powerful foes,
I prepare to celebrate and thrill,
Singing and making music
To You, Yah!

Listen, Yah, to the sound of my cry
And, being kind, answer me.
My heart has said:
I turn to seek You,
Your Presence is what I beg for.
Don't hide Your Face from me.
Don't just put me down,
You, who have been my helper
Don't abandon me, don't forsake me,
God, my support.
Though father and mother have left me
You, Yah, will hold me securely.

Please teach me Your way
And guide me on the straight path.
Discourage those who defame me.
False witnesses stood up against me,
Belching out violence.
Don't let me become
The victim of my foes.

[I would not have survived]
If I had not hoped that I would yet see
Yah's goodness fully alive on Earth.

So friend, you too, hope to Yah.
Be sturdy!
And make strong your heart!
And most of all – keep hoping to Yah.

Psalm 67
A psalm for all the peoples of the planet

God, bless us with grace!
Let Your loving Face shine on us!
We want to get to know Your way
here on Earth,
Seeing how Your help is given
to every group of people.

Oh, how the various peoples will thank You,
All of them will sing and be grateful.

Many people will be joyous and sing
When You will set them right with forthrightness.
And the peoples, as You direct them, will cheer You.

Oh how the various peoples will thank You
All of them will sing, be grateful.

The Earth will give her harvest.
Such blessings come from God, yes from our God!

Bless us God,
All the ends of the Earth will esteem You!

Psalm 90
Moses, a God's man at prayer:

Master! You are our home
each time we are born again.

Before mountains emerged,
before Earth and Space were born,
from Cosmos to Cosmos,
You are God.
You bring us, poor weak ones,
to death's door
and you urge us:
"Return, Adam's kin!"

In your gaze,
a millennium is as yesterday gone,
like a watch at night.

You flooded us with sleep.
Morning had us as wilted hay.

Blossoming with dawn,
only to change at dusk,
all wilted and dry.

Your wrath makes us panic.
Your anger confuses us.

For all our crooked places
are open to Your gaze.
Our hidden stirrings,
are visible to Your inner light.

We note all our days,
fleeing from Your ire.
Our years are fading
like a fleeting thought.

Our life span's days,
are seventy years,
and if hardy, eighty years.
Their gain is struggle and offense.
Soon we are chopped down,
dispersed and gone.
Who can estimate
the extent of Your rage?
Fear of Your ire paralyzes us.
Make us aware enough
to treasure our days;
a wise heart brings vision.

How long it seems – Relent!
I am in Your service.
Become reconciled with me.

Gladden us, no less
than You made us suffer,
those years we endured such harm.

Oh that we could see
Your design clearly,
Your grandeur in our children.

May Your kindly Presence, Lord,
be ever pleasant for us.
May our hands' efforts
achieve their aim.
Please let our efforts
result in good.

Psalm 91
A Song against Evil Spirits

In concealment You dwell,
Most High, Almighty,
You linger in the shadow.

I say to You YHVH
You are both my safe haven,
My bastion holding me.
I must trust You my God.
You save me from entrapment,
from putrid scourge.
You cover me under Your shelter.
You keep me safe under Your wings.
I am protected by Your truth.

(I am assured by You.)

Do not panic
facing night's terror,
a bullet shot in broad daylight,
a blight creeping in the murky dark,
a wasting plague at high noon.

You will not be harmed
though a thousand fall near you,
a myriad at your right hand.

You just look steadfastly ahead
and you will see
how malice will
get its rebuke.

Yes, You, YHVH are my defense.
I am at home with You,
high beyond reach.

(You assure me.)
No mishap will befall you.
Your tent will be safe from harm.

Angels are appointed to care
and watch over you
wherever you are.

They will bear you high
on their hands.
You will not strike your foot
against a stone.
Snakes and wildcats
will avoid you.
Lions and serpents
will get out of your way.

(You assure me.)
Because you long for Me
I will rescue you.
I will raise you up
because you know My Name.

When you call Me
I will answer you.
I will free you and esteem you.

I will make you content
with your life span
and I will have you witness
how I bring deliverance.

Psalm 104

Bless YAH, breath of mine.
YAH, my God, You are so vast and great
All veiled in pride and glory!

You are wrapped in Light.
The sky You spread like a sheet.

Your upper chambers are water roofed
As You bestride clouds.
You waft on the wings of wind.

The breezes You send are Your aides,
Your helpers - blazing flames.
You founded Earth so sound
To outlast time itself.

The abyss You covered like a mantle;
Water! On mountains rests.

You sound a roar and they flee.
Your thunder makes them shake.

Mountains high and valleys low
Their places they assume.

You set them limits they cannot pass
Never again to flood the land.

Springs - flow into brooks
and snake between the mountains.

All the wild of field drink there.
The beasts slake there their thirst.

By their shores dwell birds that soar,
Sounding calls through leaves and reeds.

You drench the hills
from Your Upper Chambers.
From your hands' produce
The Earth is filled.

You grow fodder for the tamed beasts
And herbs with human labor,
To bring forth bread from Earth.

And wine - to delight the sad ones,
And oil - that softens skin,
And bread - that sustains the weak.

Even the trees you sate with sap,
The cedars You planted on the Lebanon.
There birds find their nesting.
There storks find homes to rest.
Antelopes bound on the heights.
Marmots hide behind rocks.

The Moon pulls tides and seasons.
The sun knows where to set.

You darken dusk to night,
The forest's night life stirs.

The big cats cry for prey,
Praying to God for their food.

They return at the rising of the sun
To crouch once more in lairs,

While humans go out to work,
To their toil - up to night.

How many things You do!
So wisely are they made.
All Earth at your command.

This vast sea beyond all grasp,
Countless are the creatures in her,
Tiny ones and giant whales.

There go stately ships,
This Leviathan You shaped
To play and romp therein.

They all rely on Your care,
To feed them well each time.

You give to them and they take it.
Your hand's gifts sate them well.
You hide your face, they panic.
You recall their breaths, they die.
They return to their dust.
You send your spirit
And they are re-created.
So, too, You renew life on Earth.

Let Your glory, Yah, fill time and space.
Take Joy, O Yah, in what You do!

You look at Earth and she trembles,
Hills You touch and they smoke.

I live Your song, my Yah,
My Yah, I am Your tune.

Let my talking give You joy.
I am so happy, my Yah!

I wish no sin existed on Earth
All wickedness were gone.

Bless that Yah, my soul, my breath.

HALLELU-YAH!

Psalm 139
Conductor - David's Prayer set to Music

Yah! You have scanned me
And discerned me.
You know when I am relaxed or agitated.
From afar You comprehend my fantasies.
You design my conduct and my repose.
You direct my paths so I can manage.

Before my mouth opens
You know what I am about to say.
You have shaped my past and my future.
Your hand rests gently on my shoulder.
All this awes my awareness.
It is beyond my skills to fathom.

Whereto can I withdraw from Your spirit?
Flee from facing You?

If I would mount up to Heaven
There are You.
If I make my bed in Hell
You are there, too.

Soaring on the wings of the dawn,
To find shelter in the setting sun,
It would be Your hand,
that would carry me,
Your right hand, holding me safe.

If I want to find oblivion in darkness,
Trading light for darkness,
To You, it would still not be dark.
Night is as bright as day for You.
Dark and light – the same in Your sight.

You have designed my innards,
shaped me in my mother's womb .

I am overcome with thanks
At your awesome wonders,
Your astonishing works,
Of which my soul is aware.

My essence is not hidden from You,
Who have made me in concealment,
Who has knitted me beneath the surface.

Your eyes have seen me as embryo.
My days are all inscribed in Your ledger –
Days not yet shaped –
each one of them counted.

How precious are Your stirrings
in me, Oh God!
How powerful their impact!
I can't number them —
beyond all sand grains.
When I emerge from my reflection
I am still with You.

If You, God, would only rid us
of our evil!
If only the cruelty would disappear!
And defiance of You vanish,
Forgiveness overtaking enmity!

I detest hatred of You – Yah!
Quarrelsomeness repels me.
I loathe hostility to the utmost.

God! I open myself to Your scrutiny.
Know what is in my heart.
Examine and know my longings.
See and remove any defiance from me
And guide me in the way
that serves Your intent for our Earth.

IX

And in Conclusion

While working on *The Holistic Haggadah*[53] , for which Reb Zalman contributed much of the translation, I approached him with a request to translate the concluding statement that ends the seder ritual. He was very busy and just couldn't find the time to work on these last few lines. But one evening, when we were attending a prayer event organized by the local Jewish Renewal community in a Methodist Church, I approached Reb Zalman again. He asked for a pen, found a small scrap of paper in his pocket, went to the side of the room and, without reference to the Hebrew, wrote out this spontaneous translation. It is with that sense of his genius that I wish to end this volume. May you be blessed. — Editor

Nirtzah

We conclude the Seder ritual as a rite,
As we understood it and as it was beyond our understanding.
Just as we were blessed to experience it,
May we be blessed to realize it.
Ominous One, who dwells on High,
Raise us up, as a nation of renown.
May You soon gather Your beloved throng,
Redeemed we come to Zion, singing You our song.

NEXT YEAR IN JERUSALEM
NEXT YEAR IN THE REBUILT JERUSALEM
NEXT YEAR IN EARTHLY JERUSALEM —
A REFLECTION OF THE HEAVENLY JERUSALEM

---

53   *The Holistic Haggadah.* Michael L. Kagan. (Urim Publications, 2004)

While Isaiah has given us the thrice holy hymn of the angels in the sacred tongue of Hebrew, the Rabbis, making sure that everyone would understand a more human sanctification, gave us this Kaddish in the local vernacular Aramaic.

In time this prayer, an affirmation of our loyalty to God, has been attached to portions of the prayers to be recited by the mourners. This is to help the deceased in the afterlife and the grieving person to become reconciled to the reality of death.

Kaddish

May Your glory
Be known in its immensity
And experienced in holiness
In this world
Which You constantly create.
May Your Majesty
Be manifested to us all
And help us
To make ready Your redemption,
To bring about the messianic future.
May this come soon,
In our very lifetime,
And in the lifetime
Of the entire house of Israel;
Let us say – Amen!

Yes, we all want to see
Your great and awesome name
Honored and proclaimed
Everywhere and forever – Amen!

With every kind of adoration,
Celebration, exultation
That we can offer Your sacred reputation –
You are the Holy One of Blessing.
But far beyond all expressions,
Of gratitude and adoration,
Hymn and praise,
That we, of this world, can offer You,
To this we say – Amen!

May abundant peace descend from heaven
And suffuse our life with goodness,
And the life of all of Israel;
And let us say – Amen!

You God, who easily makes peace in heaven,
Make peace for us here on earth –
That is a little more difficult –
Peace for us, for Israel
And for all sentient beings on earth –
Amen!

X

The Master's Voice

There is a wonderful function available on Skype that allows one party to a video-call see the computer screen of the other. This is how Reb Zalman and I worked putting the final touches to the manuscript and finishing off the personal introduction notes to each poem. He dictated and I typed, and he would watch my screen while I sat in Jerusalem and he sat in Boulder. And then during one working session I asked him to read one of the poems, or maybe he just started reading it spontaneously, I don't remember, and the idea of including an audio dimension to the work was born. It is one thing to read the words of these beautifully translated soul prayers, it is another to hear Reb Zalman himself recite and sing them.

These recordings were not done in the studio under perfect conditions with sophisticated microphones and complicated mixers. They were made over Skype using a Skype recorder and edited using a simple audio editor. The intention is not to take away the centrality of the written word but rather to add the voice of the Master for the sake of posterity and inspiration. So the recordings are as they are. Two of them (*Niggun* of the Ba'al Shem Tov (p. 145) and Words of Reb Yosef Yitzhak to the Melody of Reb Mikheleh (p. 147) were copied from a pre-existing disk – *At the Rebbe's Table* Vol 2.[54] Two more were taken from *Your Glory Shines*,[55] a collection of traditional and original songs designed to help in the process of T'shuva – encountering God in the mood of the High Holidays. These two are: *Ana B'Khoah* (p. 40) sung to the arousing melody of the Rhizhiner Rebbe; and "We Are As Clay" (p. 103) which includes a short introduction on how to face the Gates of Turning.

Then there is the finale. In the text we end, as on all occasions in Jewish prayer, with the *Kaddish* – the Sanctification of the Holy Name (p. 206). But I decided that I wanted to leave the

---

54   *At the Rebbe's Table – Rabbi Zalman Schachter-Shlomi's Legacy of Songs and Melodies* (2007) collected, transcribed and edited by Eyal Rivlin with Netanel Miles-Yepez.

55   *Your Glory Shines* (1982) with accompaniment on guitar by Neil Seidel.

reader/listener with something that I consider even greater – the sound of the Shofar – the holy ram's horn. But not just any Shofar and not just the traditional notes heard on Rosh Hashanah but something more, so much more – a primordial sound that reaches beyond the structure, beyond the self, beyond all else to the very gates, nay, the Throne itself. Read the poem "*Abba, Abba*, Have Pity" (p. 93) then listen to the sounds that Reb Zalman, together with Paul Horn on the flute, manages to squeeze out of this morphogenetic instrument that resonates with the sound of the beginning and end of time.[56]

To hear or download the audio files of Reb Zalman chanting prayer/poems from this book go to the webpage
www.gaonbooks.com/AllBreathingLife.

Michael L. Kagan

---

56   "Paul Horn stepped down from his seat and added his flute to the shofar, guitars and voices. Not only did the entire room sing, the entire room improvised, as one being managing to incorporate the disparate sources of sound. At first somewhat disorganized, the sounds tentatively reached for one another, found a joyful union, and then swelled and ebbed with their own life, changing tempo and pitch and timbre and volume and still remaining together through some supra-rational communication. By the end of the evening there was literally no "audience," as everyone in the room had gathered around the rabbis on the stage to sing and dance in still closer communication." Recorded at the Transpersonal Conference in Bombay in 1982 with Reb Zalman, Reb Shlomo Carlebach and Paul Horn.

Other Gaon Books on Spirituality

Schachter-Shalomi, Zalman and Netanel Miles-Yepez, 2011.
A Hidden Light: stories and teachings of early ḤaBaD and Bratzlav Hasidism. ISBN: 9781935604204. Cloth and Paper. 520 pages.

Kantrowitz, Min, 2010. *Counting the Omer: A Kabbalistic Meditation Guide.* ISBN: 9781935604006. Paper. 244 pages.

Vorhand, Susan, 2009. *The Mosaic Within: An Alchemy of Healing Self and Soul.* ISBN: 9780982065730. Cloth and Paper. 280 pages.

Paloma, Vanessa, 2007. *Mystic Siren: Woman's Voice in the Balance of Creation.* ISBN: 9780977751457. Paper. 56 color images. 80 pages.

Abella Ballen, Gloria, Forthcoming Winter 2011-12. *The Power of the Hebrew Alphabet.* ISBN: 9781935604259.

www.gaonbooks.com

CPSIA information can be obtained at www.ICGtesting.com
Printed in the USA
BVOW072323141211

278387BV00001B/40/P

9 781935 604297